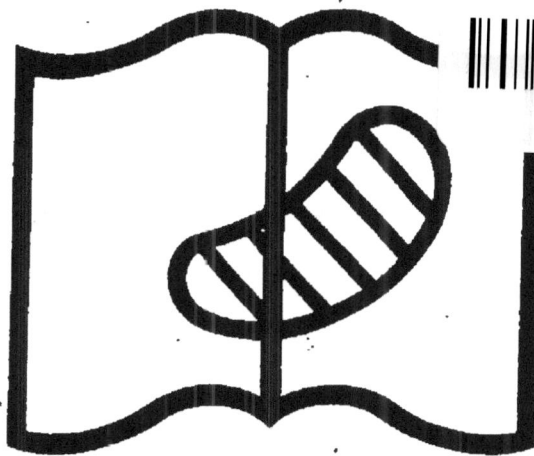

Original illisible

NF Z 43-120-10

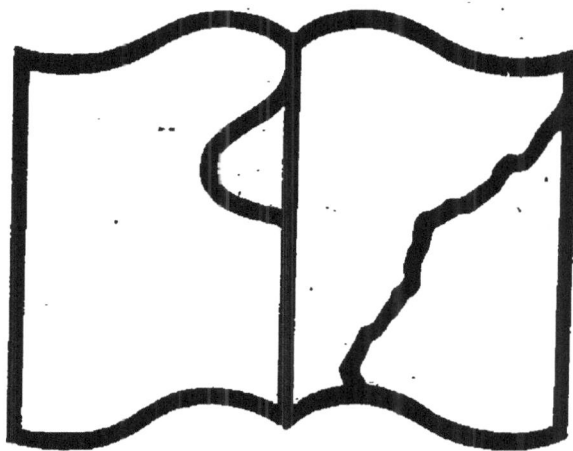

Texte détérioré — reliure défectueuse

NF Z 43-120-11

"VALABLE POUR TOUT OU PARTIE
DU DOCUMENT REPRODUIT".

THE

AMERICANS

IN

PARIS

WITH NAMES AND ADDRESSES, SKETCH OF AMERICAN ART
LISTS OF ARTISTS AND PICTURES, AND MISCELLANEOUS
MATTER OF INTEREST TO AMERICANS ABROAD.

(By Albert Sutliffe

I cannot rest from travel. I will drink
Life to the lees.

PARIS:
PRINTED FOR THE AUTHOR AND EDITOR.
1887.

T. Symonds, Printer.
90 rue Rochechouart, Paris.

Engel, Binder,
91 rue du Cherche-Midi.

" Willing Exiles."

PREFACE.

. , ...

The preface of the book aims rather to explain its object than to excuse its being. The Americans as a people have had a sort of kinship with the French since the two nations made common cause against the English during the War of Independence. There have since been occasional disagreements but the intimacy then formed has never ceased. Americans personally have been an important element of Paris society for more than fifty years though they could hardly be said to form a colony till the Empire when the surroundings of the Imperial Court and the social life and movement of the capital were such as were best calculated to attract and retain them. They are not now so numerous, but they form a colony in a strictly social sense which can be said of the foreign residents in Paris of no other nationality. This colony is annually increased by a less permanent element consisting of students of art and music of whom there are now several hundred and the number is constantly increasing. The aggregate of American travellers who come to France every year is only excelled by that of England for which there are geographical reasons. A peculiar interest attaches to the first men who represented the young Republic of the West at the French Court. They were the great figures of our epic period and their shadows lie grandly across the intervening century. This is the first attempt to give historical continuity to this American life, to impart to it an individuality, to tell who the Americans in Paris have been and are, and to show what relations they bear to one another and to the complex life about them. If the result is not always satisfactory it is because the means have been inadequate. Books needed for consultation were not in the best Paris libraries, or if there, were not accessible. Some points of personal interest have for this reason been lost sight of. Other matters essentially personal or social have been briefly alluded to or ignored because their nearness to the present time made their treatment difficult or delicate. Many names omitted from the Calling and Address List from errors in transcription or because not furnished in time will be found in a supplemental list at the close of the volume. The work is offered to the public without further explanation. Its defects must be considered as essential to its character. As it stands, with its historical sketch, its personal lists, its rules for social guidance and its social memoranda, it is thought that it will prove of interest and value to every American resident of Paris.

THE EDITOR.

TABLE OF CONTENTS.

AMERICAN TRAVELLERS IN EUROPE.

Travel having always been dependent on convenient means of international communication is a comparatively modern diversion. As such it is enjoyed by the people of different nationalities according to the general diffusion of intelligence and the individual distribution of wealth, the last being the chief reason and furnishing approximatively the ratio of those who go abroad. We have here the primary answer to the question " Why do Americans travel so much?" though there are other causes. In no other country in the world are the middle-classes so often possessed of independent means. Nowhere else is education so widely diffused. The true American is an active not to say a mercurial being. His normal existence is one of movement. He is accustomed to travel from his youth. There is much to be seen without transcending the boundaries of his native land, and not a little in the great diversity of manners and customs essential to so broad a land and so great a people that strikes the person going from one extreme of it to the other as something more than novel, as in reality strange and foreign. Such is the impression made upon the native of one of the Atlantic States by a first visit to the Pacific coast. A country that spans a continent and abuts on the two greatest oceans of the world is necessarily one of broad horizons and magnificent distances. To the average American there is no mystery beyond the horizon. And he has been so accustomed to see distance annihilated that it is of little consequence to him whether the space which it seems desirable to traverse comprises so many thousand miles of land or a like extent of ocean. Paris is no

2

farther from New York than San Francisco and it costs less to
go there. Then, why should he think it a great feat of travel to
come to Paris? And when at Paris the map of Europe is unrolled
before him not containing a single railroad route half as long as
any one of his own transcontinental lines, nor any longer than
any one of those that connect the Great Lakes with the shores of
the Gulf of Mexico. The English are great travellers, not always
for pleasure but made so by their extensive commerce and the
requirements of their numerous colonies. Were England without
colonial dependencies, and as far from the great highways of
modern travel as the United States, the class of her citizens who go
abroad would comprise few besides her nobility and her moneyed
aristocracy. It is her petty *bourgeoisie,* her tradesmen and her commercial employes who swell the ranks of continental travel during
the vacation season, the reasonable price at which circular tickets
are issued and a discreet economy enabling them to do the Rhine,
Belgium and Holland, or a part either of France, Italy or Spain,
for a comparatively small amount of money. It is nearly seven
thousand miles from San Francisco to Paris, yet almost as
many Americans come to Paris annually from that city as
from Edinburgh. Distances from all parts of the United
States to Europe being considered there is no people in
the world who travel so much as the Americans. They
go abroad in great numbers without thinking of the in-
conveniences of ocean travel, and having arrived in Europe,
as they have come so far and it may never be possible to
come again they sometimes feel compelled to make the tour of
more countries than can profitably be visited in the time at their
disposal. It is the fault of circumstances rather than a lack of
intelligent appreciation, or the accumulated nervous force they
have brought with them from a climate overcharged with
electricity.

The Travellers' Mecca. Few Americans come to Europe without visiting Paris. It is a travellers' Mecca exacting of its devotees neither fanaticism nor special faith. The exceptions are usually those who come and return by the Amsterdam or Hamburg lines. Most of the travel comes by way of England, but the new steamers of the Transatlantic Line have their share. The majority of tourists come in spring, because for the greater part of Europe, the summer and early autumn are most agreeable, and in all respects most convenient. If they come by any one of the English lines they spend a short time in London. Then they cross to Paris with a view to spending a part of May and June there before scattering to the French watering-places, Switzerland, the Tyrol, Norway and Sweden, Belgium, Holland, the North of Germany, and parts of Austria. In all these countries travelling is easy and comfortable in summer. Norway has grown greatly in favor of late years. It has become a fashionable resort not only to Americans and English who discovered its merits some years ago, but to the French who rarely go to Germany, and so find the tourist field limited. There exists an unreasonable prejudice against visiting Italy in summer, and especially Rome which is haunted by the grim specter of the fever. The summers about the Mediterranean are warm, but in most parts of Italy the nights have usually a refreshing coolness, and the fever is what no adult person who exercises caution need fear. There is a considerable number of Americans who, owing to business, can come but once to Europe, and then only in the summer. Rome is to them the city of their dreams, but they do not go there because they fear the heat and the fever. There are others who come to Europe several summers in succession, and never get further south in Italy than Lake Como or Milan. They labor under a delusion. They should see Rome and—not die of the fever—but have the longing of a life-time satisfied, and their European tour properly rounded and finished by a vision of the noblest and most unique objects that Europe has to offer to the sight-seer. A great part of Spain may be comfortably seen in summer, and even Tangiers, Algiers and Egypt may be visited during the warm season with less discomfort than attends a railroad journey in August in the Northern States.

Ebb and Flow of Travel. The autumn influx of American trave has a different meaning, and, it may be added, a less ruddy complexion, for an important part of it is composed of those persons who are fleeing from the cold winters of the Northern States to seek a more congenial climate at Cannes, Nice, Mentone, on the Riviera, or at Florence, Rome and Naples. This southward pilgrimage which files through Paris with the regularity of the seasons when the autumn winds begin to blow is not entirely moved by sanitary instincts. It includes a large proportion of pleasure-seekers who object to a hard winter on principle, and prefer sunshine, genial airs and unrestricted freedom of movement. Further than this, though Italy has her monuments at all seasons, life stagnates from the end of May to October in her large cities. Winter along the littoral of the midland sea is a season of commercial activity as well as of personal enjoyment. It is this friction of the best individual elements of civilized nations gathered in certain centres, this social life that has the brilliant color of southern lands and seas that attracts the class of Americans, and it is not a small one, who are able to embroider their lives so heavily with pleasure as almost to conceal its sombre background. By the first of December the hotels of Paris are comparatively deserted, and those of the French littoral, of the Riviera, of Florence, Rome and about the Bay of Naples are full, and a large proportion of the guests are from the United States. Thenceforth, during the winter the travel is only occasional. It has no longer the character of a caravan. But there has been in the meantime a counter-current of tourists gathered from all parts of central and southern Europe who are passing through Paris on their way to America. In spring there is the same undertow sweeping back across the Atlantic the greater part of those who have spent the winter in the south of Europe.

There is twice every year this ebb and flow, these currents that meet each other in Paris. There are also cross-currents conducting to foreign capitals, or into by-ways of travel that have their importance. There are Americans who spend years in Europe, the winter on the Mediterranean, the summer in Paris, London, or elsewhere in the north. Others are the merest waifs of travel driven hither and thither by chance winds and currents, making some large city their headquarters and spending most of their time in short visits to localities that have a temporary interest. And so their life passes till this constant change of place becomes a necessity, a fever even, and they find that like Ulysses they "cannot rest from travel," but must go on "drinking life to the lees." There are not only Americans who, like a certain character mentioned in the Book of Job, spend their whole lives in going to and fro in Europe, and walking up and down in it, not neglecting the north of Africa and Palestine, but who have made the tour of the world several times and who intend to perform that feat several times more. Travel is no doubt a most excellent thing. It gives refinement and finish to mind and manners. But it was probably never intended by a superintending Providence, which acts the part of a life assurance company toward the migratory being who undergoes so many perils by land and water that it degenerate into a disease. It is pleasant, nevertheless, to believe that the malady can never be more than exceptional and that the benefits of travel must always far outweigh all the evil effects arising from its abuses.

Special Characteristics. The peculiarities and character of American tourists are sometimes called in question. As the United States has had an entirely different origin, and a different development from any other nation, and exists at present under political, social and literary conditions unlike those of any other country, this is not surprising. If we could pass the fine-tooth comb which plays its part in American slang delicately over the American travelling public, and send to Europe only our most cultivated millionaires, the combined effect of their gold and good manners would be to gladden the hearts of French landlords and delight the best European social circles. Or if by the practice of a similar electicism we could send only our men of science and literature, who are at the same time refined witty and erudite, the impression would no doubt be gratifying, and gratifying only. If we were able to pursue a similar course in other respects, only sending our best sample lots abroad and keeping the commoner qualities of our social wares at home, the criticisms we hear, and we cannot say that they are often offensive, would be radically changed in tone. But while Russia furnishes tourists only from her aristocratic and educated classes, and England travelling specimens of every class, and is judged by the best alone, the United States, knowing no rank and admitting the equality of all men is estimated on that leveling principle, and finds her worst often taken for her best by people who do not understand her institutions, and do not look beneath the surface to find reasons. American travellers who have sufficient means come pell-mell to Europe. There is no winnowing of the chaff from the grain. Those who were poor yesterday and are rich to-day jostle the scions of families whose wealth has come down to them for many generations. There are gentlemen of leisure who come to spend a year or two in sauntering about the Continent. On the same steamer is the salaried man who comes to pass a vacation of two months. There are with the crowd farmers, mechanics, business men and adventurers, with a few college professors, clergymen, artists, students, authors, and journalists, the literary class being small, for most of them can ill afford an interruption of their duties lasting several months, a loss to which would have to be added the expenses of the tour. Taken as they average no American in Europe need be ashamed of his compatriots. They are shrewd observers, agreeable travelling companions, and as a rule kind and courteous. If rich they are often needlessly lavish to servants to the great annoyance of those in moderate circumstances who follow in their footsteps. There are those among them who, impatient of the exactions of landlords and petty dealers, and the impertinence of domestics, give way to unseemly bursts of passion. This happens to travellers of all nations. They are the exceptions. As a rule they bear with equanimity the discomforts of the migratory life they are obliged to lead. They supplement whatever knowledge they may chance to have of interesting scenes and objects with guides and guidebooks in the usual manner, and as to the night-side of the life of great cities their desire to see it has scarcely as yet attained the abnormal development characteristic of the European nobleman. To say more than this would be to intimate that the American traveller in Europe is a being of specialized instincts of a type so eccentric as to be at once recognized and classified apart from the tourists of other nations, which would be absurd.

HISTORICAL RESUME.

The Americans before the Revolution knew little more of France than its name, and with its name they associated the prejudices they had inherited from their English ancestors. They were too poor to indulge in travel. Occasionally sons of wealthy families finished their studies in England and made a short tour of the Continent bringing back from France only strengthened prejudices against a people whose language they did not understand and whose manners impressed them as in the highest degree artificial. The Colonists had fought the wars of England against the French in Canada and in the West, and war leaves its bitter memories to future generations. They were Protestant to the core, and they remembered the Huguenots, many of whose descendants were among them, and could not forget St. Bartholomew and the Revocation of the Edict of Nantes. In a word they were provincial Americans and not the travelled and cosmopolitan Americans of to-day. The only American colonist who came to France in pre-Revolutionary times with the idea that the country had something to teach him was the great surgeon, Benjamin Rush, who, after passing some time in the hospitals of London and Edinburgh, visited those of Paris. What would he have thought, could he have seen the horde of American students of art and medicine who annually invade the continental capitals !

Benjamin Franklin.
The Revolution changed the current of American thought in regard to Europe. The paternal and fraternal feeling that had prevailed between England and her most important trans-Atlantic colonies was transformed during the long struggle into a sullen resentment. There are no hatreds so bitter as those between members of like race, of similar religious faith, or of the same family. The assistance which France had rendered assured the permanent friendship of the new nation. Hitherto citizens of the two countries had only known each other on the battlefields of the northern and western frontier. They were now to mingle in more intimate social relations the way to it having been paved by traditional hostility between France and England, and the pressing need in which the Americans stood of some powerful foreign alliance. Fortunately the good genius that presided at the birth of the new Republic had provided the man for the hour—Benjamin Franklin. The heart of the French nation had been gradually preparing for just such a critical period for such an outburst of liberal feeling. The French mind was fallow for the seed that the wise western husbandman had to scatter. The reaction from the artificial period of Louis Fifteenth had continued and gathered head during that of Louis Sixteenth, so that plain Benjamin Franklin whose fame had preceded him and who came in a merely political capacity was enabled to win a social triumph more brilliant, if not more substantial, than his diplomatic successes. The impression he made on the cultivated classes is admirably expressed in the following passage from the French historian, Charles Lacretelle : "By the effect which Franklin produced in France, one might say that he fulfilled his mission, not with a court, but with a free people. Diplomatic etiquette did not permit him often to hold interviews with the ministers, but he associated with the distinguished personages who directed public opinion. Men imagined they saw in him a sage of antiquity come back to give austere lessons and generous examples to the moderns. They personified in

him the Republic of which he was the representative and the legislator. They regarded his virtues as those of his countrymen, and even judged of their physiognomy by the imposing and serene traits of his own. Happy was he who could gain admittance to see him in the house which he occupied at Passy. The venerable old man, it was said, joined to the demeanor of Phoçion the spirit of Socrates. Courtiers were struck with his natural dignity, and discovered in him the profound statesman. Young officers impatient to signalize themselves in another hemisphere came to interrogate him respecting the military condition of the Americans, and when he spoke to them with deep concern and manly frankness of the recent defeats which had put his country in jeopardy, this only excited in them a more ardent desire to join and assist the republican soldiers. After this picture it would be useless to trace the history of Franklin's negociations with the Court of France. His virtues and his renown negotiated for him, and before the second year of his mission no one conceived it possible to refuse fleets and armies to the compatriots of Franklin."

Paris expectant. Franklin crossed the ocean in a sailing vessel, which after a long and perilous voyage arrived safely at Nantes having several times narrowly escaped capture by British cruisers. His coming had been eagerly expected, and he received a welcome immediately on landing. In a letter dated at Nantes he writes : "I find it generally supposed that I am sent to negotiate, and that opinion appears to give great pleasure, if I can judge by the extreme civilities I meet with from numbers of the principal people who have done me the honor to visit me." From Nantes he went directly to Paris where he took an apartment in the Rue de l'Université. A few days after he removed to Passy where he remained till he returned to America. Madame du Deffand, then a very old woman, was among those on the *qui vive*. She writes to her friend, Horace Walpole : "The object of Franklin's visit is still problematical, and what is more singular no one can tell whether or not he is actually in Paris. For three or four days past, it has been said every morning that he has arrived, and every evening that he has not come." She adds in a letter written shortly afterwards : " Dr. Franklin arrived in town yesterday. He slept the night before at Versailles. He was accompanied by two of his grandsons, one seven and the other seventeen years old, and by his friend, Mr. Penet." Franklin found Mr. Deane, one of his coadjutors, at Paris, awaiting him. Mr. Lee, another of the American commissioners, came the next day. The last took charge of the negotiations with Spain and Prussia, which he managed without success, and after some years in Europe, having created by his jealous and irritable disposition considerable embarassment for Franklin he returned to America. It is not necessary to give in detail the history of Franklin's negotiations with the French Court. He came to obtain ships and men and money which were furnished in one form or another, secretly at first, and openly after England having remonstrated and then threatened, felt herself at last compelled to declare war. The applications made to him by young men anxious to fight the battles of freedom were so numerous as to be painfully annoying since, though he appreciated the spirit in which they were made, he could do nothing. There were no places at his disposal, and to recommand *en masse* would have been utterly without avail. His letter commending Lafayette to the kind offices of his countrymen is, nevertheless, worthy of preservation in this place :

The Marquis de Lafayette, a young nobleman of great family connexions here, and great wealth, is gone to America in a ship of his own, accompanied by some officers of distinction, in order to serve in our armies. He is exceedingly beloved, and everybody's good wishes attend him. We cannot but hope he may meet with such a reception as will make the country and his expedition agreeable to him. Those who censure it as imprudent in him, do, nevertheless, applaud his spirit, and we are satisfied that the civilities and respect that may be shown him will be serviceable to our affairs here, as pleasing not only to his powerful relations and to the Court, but to the whole French nation. He has left a beautiful young wife and for her sake particularly, we hope that his bravery and ardent desire to distinguish himself will be a little restrained by the General's prudence, so as not to permit his being hazarded much, except on some important occasion.

A Philosopher's Associates. Franklin was a travelled man for his epoch. He had spent two years in England and been twice in Paris, where thoroughly imbued with English prejudices he found nothing to his liking. His present visit was on an entirely different basis. He came in a spirit of friendship. He came asking favors, and brought with him a more catholic judgment. He was now prepared to appreciate the fine qualities of the people whose goodwill he sought to gain and they, for many reasons, were prepared to admire him. The record of his social experiences can, therefore, never cease to be interesting to Americans. He was on the most friendly terms with the best people who lived about him at Passy. Among the eminent men whom he met often were Turgot, Buffon, D'Alembert, Condorcet, La Rochefoucauld, Cabanis, Le Roy, Raynal, Mably. He met, at the house of Madame Denis, Voltaire, who had come to Paris to pass the last few days of his life. Voltaire addressed him in English, and was continuing the conversation in that language when Madame Denis interrupted him by saying that Franklin understood French, and the rest of the company would like to know the subject of discussion. Voltaire replied, " Excuse me, my dear, I have the ambition to show that I am not unacquainted with the language of a Franklin." The two old men met once more at the public *séance* of the Academy, and shooks hands in the English manner. The entire audience rose, and applauded vociferously, and cried out, " Not like the English. Like the French." This meant that they should exchange a friendly kiss. They complied, and then seated themselves side by side where they remained the cynosure of all eyes till the close of the meeting. Voltaire died a year or two afterwards. Franklin appeared at Court on the same footing as the ambassadors of foreign nations. By his simplicity, his goodness, and the sincerity of his character he quickly gained the sympathy of everyone. As a historian says of him, this printer-physician, this republican philosopher, clad in thick cloth, in his fur-cap, his long grey hair falling about his shoulders, in the midst of elegant and refined people, dressed in velvet, silk and lace, astonished by his unassuming manners after having excited astonishment by his discoveries. He was fêted. He became the mode. Portraits of him were sold everywhere in the form of busts, stamps, engravings, medallions, cameos and on bracelets and snuff-boxes. They made epigrams on him, one of which was to the effect that he had stolen the thunder from heaven and the scepter from tyrants. Though all the people of Passy vied in their attentions to him he was most at home in the family of M. Brillon. The house of Madame Helvetius at Auteuil, was a favorite resort. This lady who was now a widow, and advanced in years, had associated in her youth with the most celebrated wits and literary men of the day. How his life passed politically and socially from day to day at his home at Passy is suggested by the following brief extracts from his diary: "To-day M. Dupont, Inspector of Customs, came to talk to me about the free port of L'Orient." "The Pope's Nuncio called and acquainted me that the Pope had at my recommendation appointed Mr. John Carroll, superior of the Catholic clergy in America." "M. Franks dined with me in company with M. Helvetius, Abbé de la Roche, M. Cabanis, and an American captain." "MM. Mirabeau and Champfort came," and so on through many pages. This adulation and the political success he achieved, had its effect. He accommodated his dress to the fashions of the period. He forgot the opinions regarding the French that he had expressed on former visits. That their manners were artificial, that they used snuff to excess, that they were the slaves of fashion, were defects far outweighed by the brilliant qualities and solid nature that a closer acquaintance revealed to him. In 1779 he wrote :

I am charmed with what you say of French politeness, and the honest manners which are shown by the officers and crew of the fleet of this country. In this respect, the French far surpass the English, I find it the most amiable nation in the world to live with. The Spaniards are commonly considered cruel, the English haughty, the Scotch insolent, the Dutch avaricious, etc. But the French seem to me to have no grave defect. They have certain frivolities which harm no one. To dress the hair in such a manner as to be unable to put the hat on, and to be obliged, therefore, to carry it in the hand, to fill the nose with tobacco, are ridiculous habits, but are not faults. They are only the fantastic effects of the tyranny of fashion. In short there is nothing wanting to the French character necessary to the making of an agreeable or gallant man. If there are some trifles on the surface they are not to be noticed.

Return to America. This shows how completely he had been captured. Franklin went to France in 1776. While at Passy he had the assistance from time to time of Silas Deane, Arthur Lee brother of Richard Henry Lee, John Adams, and John Jay. Peace was declared by the treaty of Versailles in 1782. His work being done, he having now reached extreme old age, and his presence being needed in America, he asked to be relieved. Mr. Jay returned home in 1783, and his place was supplied by Thomas Jefferson, who arrived at Passy in 1784. The French Minister, Vergennes, said to him: "You replace Mr. Franklin, I think;" to which Jefferson replied: "I succeed Dr. Franklin. No one can replace him." Franklin left Passy the same year for home, going by way of Rouen to Havre, where he intended to embark. At Rouen he was the guest of the Archbishop. Here also he received the calls of the nobility of the neighborhood. Then having reposed himself he went on to Havre, where he left for home, followed by the polite attentions of all the people to the last, and by their good wishes to the end of his life.

Thomas Jefferson. Jefferson came to represent the new and independent nation. It was not so much assistance that he wanted as friendly co-operation while it was learning to go alone. He had a quick intellect and a mobile temperament not distantly related to the French character. He was possessed of literary tastes and aspirations, and had long desired to be near some great center of thought and culture, where he could find sympathetic companionship rare in a country where everything was as yet new and unformed. He took apartments in the "Cul-de-sac Têtebout," so-called then, though now a street connecting the grand boulevards with the Boulevard Haussmann, and furnished it in a manner extravagant for his means, and not altogether consistent with republican simplicity. He placed his daughters in a conventual school. The members of his family were Colonel Humphreys, Secretary of Legation, and Mr. Short, his private secretary, whom he held in high esteem. His first impressions of Paris were unfavorable. The people he found to be excessively immoral, and the architecture of the city the worst he had ever seen, not excepting London, or even Virginia, which he had been wont to think the worst in the world. But his opinions were soon modified, not by a worship amounting almost to adulation, like that which had been bestowed on Franklin, but by the courteous attention he received, as well as by his own good sense. A little later he found things that were admirable in French architecture as well as in French art. He sent the distinguished sculptor Houdon to Virginia to execute the statue of Washington that adorns the State house at Richmond. The question arose whether it should represent the hero in classic or modern costume. The artist preferred the former, but Jefferson insisted on the modern dress, and quoted the artists, West, Copley, Trumbull, and Brown, who appear to have been at the time in Europe, as sharing the same opinion. The admiration for French art was not then widely disseminated among American artists, nearly all of them looking to England for their inspiration and still regarding France as an artistic Nazareth out of which it was hopeless to think any good could come. How Jefferson felt toward the French later is gleaned from passages in his letters. He wrote to Madame de Corney, who was at the time in England : " I hope that when the splendor of the shops, the only thing which is worth seeing at London, has lost its novelty and charm you will sigh for Paris

and its people and will feel that you can nowhere be so happy as
in their company ***" "I am enchanted with the people and
their company," he writes elsewhere. "Here all the asperities and
rudenesses of the human mind are so perfectly effaced, that it
seems to me one could glide along all his life among them
without even being jostled." He wrote in a similar tone, but in
more general terms to friends in America :

With respect to what are termed polite manners, without sacrificing too
much the sincerity of language, I would wish my countrymen to adopt
just so much of European politeness as to be ready to make all the little
sacrifices of self which really render European manners amiable and relieve
society from the disagreeable scenes to which rudeness often subjects it.
Here it seems that a man might pass a life without encountering a single
rudeness. In the pleasures of the table they are far before us because
with good taste they unite temperance. They do not terminate the most
sociable meals by transforming themselves into brutes. I have never seen
a man drunk in France not even among the lowest of the people. Were
I to proceed to tell you how much I enjoy their architecture, sculpture,
painting and music, I should want words. It is in these arts they are
sublime. The last of them particularly is an enjoyment, the deprivation
of which with us cannot be calculated. I am almost ready to say it is
the only thing which, from my heart, I envy them and which in spite
of all the authority of the decalogue I do covet.

An opinion of Buffon. Franklin and Jefferson were Americans
in the best sense of the term. They had
the manly habit which some Americans
have now lost of standing sturdily up to defend their country and
its institutions, not right or wrong, but they held them innocent
of charges made until proved. Buffon had held that the animals
of the new world were degenerate specimens of their genus. The
Abbé Raynal had asserted that both the men and the animals of
the new world had physically retrograded. Franklin wanted the
opportunity, and one day having at dinner an equal number of
Frenchmen and Americans, the Abbé Raynal being among the
former, he brought up the subject and requested all present to

stand up. It happened that all the Frenchmen were small and all the Americans fine specimens of manhood, Franklin himself being a man of imposing appearance. The Abbé Raynal chanced to be smaller than any of his countrymen. He however refused to yield the point on the ground that any rule may have exceptions. The question of the comparative stature of the men of their nation is one that no Frenchman would now care to discuss. Jefferson took active measures to combat the opinions of Buffon. He sent to America, had a moose killed for the purpose, and its skeleton carefully prepared and brought to France in order that he might refute the assertions of the eminent naturalist. Though he found so much in French life and art that pleased him he was always ready from instinctive habit and patriotic purpose to combat everything that to his high sense of honor and decency seemed a moral heresy, or in any way false to principle. It was never possible to him to fill the place of Franklin either in a scientific or in a social capacity. As to society, though it was to use the well-worn phrase prepared to dance on the brink of a volcano, it was already beginning to decompose under the fomenting forces of the Revolution. It had already made great progress during his stay in Paris. The States General assembled at Versailles in May, 1789. The Third Estate declared itself the National Assembly and took the oath of the Tennis Hall in May. The Bastille was taken on the fourteenth of July. In August followed the Declaration of the Rights of Man. Jefferson left Paris in September of the same year and returned to Virginia by way of Havre and Cowes, leaving Mr. Short in charge of the Legation. He had asked to be recalled on account of pressing business at home, but it is probable that the prospect of the coming storm helped him to a decision.

Gouverneur Morris. Circumstances had already indicated his successor. Gouverneur Morris came to Paris in the spring of 1789, not in a diplomatic capacity, but to arrange some business for his brother

Robert Morris. He had already passed middle age. He had literary tastes and spoke French readily, an unusual accomplishment for Americans of the period. He had a previous acquaintance with Lafayette and other distinguished Frenchmen which served to open to him the doors of Paris drawing-rooms. He did not receive his credentials as minister till 1792, therefore the first three years of his life must be regarded merely from a social standpoint except that being an American statesman of reputation and having friends in the circle immediately surrounding the King his advice was frequently sought by those in high places. He met nearly every one of social eminence on terms of equality. The King listened to his counsel on critical occasions. He was regarded with great favor by the Queen Marie-Antoinette. He often met Madame de Stael in society. He greatly respected her genius but described her as looking like a chambermaid. Though a republican of the most undeniable fidelity to principle he was found too aristocratic in the salon of the Countess de Tessé where the advanced liberals met. His views were far too moderate for the extreme ideas of this company, and even for Madame de Lafayette who was displeased at his sentiments. The Duchess of Orleans, mother of M. de Beaujolais, afterwards King Louis-Philippe, was among his most intimate friends. After the days of the Terror he rendered substantial aid to both mother and son which was substantially remembered. One of his most agreeable places of resort was the salon of Madame de Flahaut, the friend of Talleyrand and Montesquieu, a clever woman influential in politics and speaking English. She knew all state secrets, and inducted him into them. She asked his advice about the formation of ministries, and the choice of ministers to foreign courts. If he disapproved of the plans of the Government he did not hesitate to say so, and his disapproval had its effect. As simple citizen he censured the course that Lafayette was pursuing. He told him that he could not act both as minister and soldier, that the cabinet he was making should be composed of men of talent and firmness. He suggested that Talleyrand should be made Minister of Finance, and strongly advised that Mirabeau should be left out. These noble republicans in France were too advanced in opinion and too timid in action to suit this cool-headed man of the new Republic of the New World. They became conservative when they saw to what excesses liberal opinions were conducting their contrymen, but it was too late. They had sown the wind, and it was inevitable they should reap the whirlwind. The most curious social experiences of Mr. Morris, and those that will now be looked back upon with the greatest interest, were those with Madame de Stael and her coterie. Here he met her father, whom she considered the alpha and omega of human wisdom but whom he, looking at the financier from his practical standpoint, regarded as he did the other friends of the King as too timid and halting. He was presented to Madame de Stael as *un homme d'esprit.* She was pleased to be complimentary and told him that his conversation must be very interesting, for she had heard him quoted everywhere. Though a woman of such solidity of genius she found it impossible to rise above the gallantries and frivolities of the time. She was pleased with her new acquaintance, and desired him to come to her Tuesday evening receptions where she met her friends in an unceremonial manner in morning toilet, which offered greater facilities to intrigue. Though personally one of the most unattractive of women she coquetted with her male visitors who pleased her, and had her lovers greatly to the grief of her less gifted husband who was in the habit of entertaining Mr. Morris with colloquial essays on the turpitude of those who were given to alienating wives from their husbands.

Appointed Minister. After Mr. Jefferson's departure the American Legation remained some years in charge of Mr. Short. During this time the appointment of Mr. Morris as minister was often mentioned, so that when offered and accepted it occasioned no surprise. Had the old regime remained no person more acceptable to the Court and the ruling classes would have been found. But everything was now changed. It was evident that if the

views of Lafayette and other liberal aristocrats were far too
advanced for him he could never please the class of politicians
and statesmen now coming into power. He had in fact already
made enemies among them by his pointed sarcasm, and he had
been warned by his friends that if he were not more discreet
his life would be in danger. The relations of France and the
United States were becoming critical even before the execution
of the King and Queen, the sober and well-regulated sympathies
of the Americans not being easily accorded to the wild vagaries
and cruel excesses of the revolutionists no matter how profoundly
they might feel for liberty in the abstract. In this fight for
independence, the Americans had only known France through
its King and nobility. To them were attached their agreeable
associations and their grateful remembrances. Their battles were,
it is true, fought with the aid of the French armies composed
of the common people, a circumstance alluded to by the Committee
of Safety in one of their manifestoes issued during the advanced
days of the Terror to which are signed the names of Robespierre
and his associates. The Convention soon after its accession to
power sent to the United States for the purpose of securing
their cooperation one Citizen Genet, whose correspondence with
the Citizen Minister of the French Republic forms an important
part of the history of the period. Citizen Genet landed at
Charleston and made a gradual progress northward visiting the
principal cities of the seaboard. He left France with the most
cordial intentions toward the new regime, but appears to have
been gradually alienated from it by the system of terror which it
inaugurated as well as by the sentiments of the Americans
who had nothing in common with the Terrorists. He was
denounced by the Committee of Safety as a traitor, but being
in America was safe from their revenge. The relations of
Mr. Morris to the Convention were not agreeable. The Minister
for Foreign Affairs endeavored to force him to recognize the
new government, but he refused, although saying at the same
time that his country would doubtless do so as soon as its
stability was secured by the approval of a majority of the

people definitively expressed. His whole course before the deposition of the King was friendly and his suggestions always listened to. He had, before becoming minister, prepared a memoir for the King which suggested a course of conduct. Madame de Stael thought it too strong, according to some reports made to him, and too weak according to others, which made him think her deceitful and led him to call her a devilish woman. She approved of nothing inconsistent with her father's views and plans. Nothing in his aristocratic associations or in his relations to royal rule was of a nature to make Morris acceptable to the Convention in an official capacity. Their hostility and their efforts to drive him from the country were therefore to be expected.

Presented to the Queen. The three years of his official life were melancholy. His reminiscences of them are fascinating. When he went to present his credentials to the King he found him already broken down in mind and body. When he was presented to the Queen she still preserved some of her former spirit, and showed her son to him with pride. She remarked that he was not yet tall. Mr. Morris expressed the hope that he would not only be tall *(grand)*, but really great *(véritablement grand)*, and she replied: "We shall do our best to make him so." He, however, thought that her conduct afterwards was not altogether discreet. The days grew darker and darker. The only pleasures of the time were those of the table, and these were saddened by the thought that some one of the convivial party gathered at the feast might never so be met again, by the news of murders or executions, or reports that the King and Queen, then imprisoned in the Temple, were expecting to be murdered at any moment. He could do nothing for them. No one could show them any courtesy in the condition in which Paris was then placed without endangering his own life. Finally, he omitted all mention of them from his diary. On going, one day, to dine with Madame de Foucault, he was informed that her *maître d'hôtel* had killed himself that morning, for which reason they dined late. Still though the times were so sad, though everybody was impoverished by the interruption of business and the stopping of pensions, a certain amount of gaiety and frivolity remained almost to the last days of the Terror. At last the Committee of Safety requested the removal of Mr. Morris in terms that hardly admitted of a refusal. Monroe arrived to replace him in 1794, but before returning home, he thought best to make a general tour of Europe. He went first to Basle, where he met Madame de Stael, and then visited several German cities, extending his journey as far as the Baltic. Returning westward, by way of Holstein, he went to London, again returning to the Continent, and visiting this time Berlin, Dresden and Vienna. While in Austria he made efforts to secure the release of Lafayette, as a private citizen, of course, his official career being ended. After some months spent at Altona, a German city not far from Hamburg, he returned to America in 1798.

Monroe's Mission. James Monroe was selected by Washington to succeed Morris, because he was an ardent sympathizer with the French Revolution. He had no aristocratic associations at Paris. Contrary to what was to be expected, it was in the South, whose social corner-stone was slavery, that were found, in the first days of the Republic, the most ardent democrats, while the New Englanders were looked upon as the real American aristocrats. So Citizen Genet, landing at Charleston, met with an enthusiastic reception, but found the people more and more unresponsive as he advanced northward along the Atlantic coast. Monroe was received with enthusiasm in Paris. He presented his letters of credence and read a written address in the hall of the Convention, around which were displayed the blended flags of France and the United States, and received from the President the *accolade*, that is to say, the fraternal embrace. For this he was severely reprimanded by Randolph, Secretary of State, who, while wishing to treat the Directory cordially did not desire the American representative to show such an amount of zeal as was likely to alienate other nations. Some of this effusiveness was attributed to the fact that Robespierre having been deposed, a greater effort was thought necessary to show the goodwill of the nation and to make the days of the Terror forgotten. Monroe was sorely tried in his attempts to soothe the wounded susceptibilities of the French. They were irritated by the evident want of sympathy on the part of the American Republic. French ports were filled with captured American vessels, and there were in Paris and other French cities hundreds of Americans who had been taken with them, or who were in one way or another, interested in their release. His task was rendered onerous by the treaty made about this time with England by Commissioner John Jay, which was thought by the French to conflict with that made by the United States with themselves in 1788. But he worked hard to accomplish the objects to which his mission was specially devoted, and had a partial success, though not sufficient to satisfy the home Government, or to prevent his recall two years later. The social life of Monroe while in Paris bore little resemblance to that of his predecessors. He interested himself with Mr. Morris in the release of Lafayette then in prison at Olmütz, and in endeavoring to render financial aid to Madame Lafayette, who was in poverty. He also tried to secure the liberation of Thomas Paine, who was in confinement at the Luxembourg then used as a prison. During his term of office several young Americans were sent to France to pursue their studies. His own son was at school at St. Germain. Monroe returned to America in 1803. He was afterwards one of the commissioners that negotiated the purchase of Louisiana which Napoleon wished to get rid of because in the case of war with England which was impending, it was a distant dependency and liable to be captured by the British navy. Its sale was greatly preferable to its dishonorable loss. The original proposition only contemplated purchasing with New Orleans but the whole territory was finally included, the price paid being $10,000,000.

Talleyrand.
Bonaparte.

Charles C. Pinckney of South Carolina succeeded Monroe. He arrived in Paris in October, 1796. The Directory refused to receive him. A commission consisting of John Marshal, of Virginia, Elbridge Gerry of Massachusetts, and Mr. Pinckney was constituted to smooth away the diplomatic difficulties that had arisen between the two countries. The Directory, represented by Talleyrand, refused to recognize it officially. The story is told without favor by the French historians who have written of the period. The situation was at one time so critical that it was thought war might break out at any moment. The United States were determined to remain neutral in the wars between France and the rest of Europe. When the terms of the treaty between the States and England were made known Talleyrand ordered the seizure of all American ships in French ports, and the capture of those found on the high seas carrying British merchandize. American commerce was by this means ruined for the moment. When the Commissioners arrived in Paris they sent Major Rutledge to Talleyrand requesting him to name a day when he could receive them. A time was fixed four days later, but the conference was postponed from time to time on various pretexts. Talleyrand used his secretary and other persons as his intermediaries. He represented the Directory as greatly incensed by the remarks made by President Adams in his message to Congress, and said that a reconciliation would be impossible till the language was modified. He insinuated that a large amount of money was needed to pave the way to a negotiation which the Commissioners said they had no authority to give. They finally offered to return to America for instructions if ships were released to enable them to make the passage. The treatment of the Commission, and the effort to extort money becoming known in Europe, the reputation of Talleyrand and the Directory suffered greatly in the eyes of all honest men. To relieve himself of the odium the minister pretended that it had been done by intriguers without his knowledge. When it was found that nothing could be accomplished the Commissioners were recalled. Pinckney and

Marshall left Paris in July 1798 and Gerry two months later. The Directory was soon afterwards succeeded by the Consulate a more stable government to which were accredited as joint envoys and ministers respectively Oliver Ellsworth of Connecticut, William Vans Murray of Maryland and William R. Davis of North Carolina. In 1803 James Monroe returned to France to negotiate with Robert R. Livingston the purchase of New Orleans which Bonaparte wished to dispose of because in case of a war with England it would inevitably be captured by the British navy. After negotiations were commenced the sale was made to include the whole territory of Louisiana then a vast unexplored wilderness whose prospective value was so imperfectly understood that the Commissioners were severely censured for having squandered the public money. The price paid was $10,000,000. Thenceforward the path of American diplomacy in France was destined to be less rugged. Robert R. Livingston was minister plenipotentiary from 1801 to 1803. Personally he was agreeable to Bonaparte who when he left Paris gave him an elegant snuff-box with a portrait of himself by Isabey.

Joel Barlow. The United States has rarely been represented at foreign courts by its literary men. The remarkable exceptions to the rule are Irving, Motley and Lowell, while journalists or professional writers of books such as John Hay, Bret Harte, Don Piatt and Alden have been, and still are, occasionally found holding consular offices or in subordinate positions at American legations. One of the earliest representatives of American literature abroad was Joel Barlow a native of Connecticut who had been a journalist and was the author of several poems of epic character that are now only remembered by name. From 1795 to 1797 he was United States Consul at Algiers where he negotiated a treaty which included Tripoli with that power. He afterwards spent several years at Paris where he amassed a large fortune in trade. Returning home he built a country-house not far from Washington which is still standing and is still remarkable for its size and magnificence. He was appointed minister to Paris in 1811, but was not destined long to fill the office. Alexander Czar of Russia had just withdrawn from the alliance made with Bonaparte at the Interview of Erfurth and thrown himself into the arms of England to whom he had opened his Black Sea ports and from whom he was receiving numerous subsidies. The continental blockade was .broken, the Russian campaign decreed. Russia was invaded in 1812, and the retreat from Moscow occurred the following winter. Barlow was asked to meet the Emperor at Wilna, but before he reached that city died at Zarnowics in Poland in December of that year. Nothing·remarkable occurred during the term of office of Minister Crawford who succeeded him.

Albert Gallatin.   One of the ablest of our early representatives to the French Government was Albert Gallatin. He was a Swiss who had come to America as a young man, had settled in the forests of Pennsylvania whence in due time he was sent to the House of Representatives. He was a Republican and bitterly hostile to the Federalists. He became Secretary of the Treasury in 1801 and held the office for twelve years. He endeavored to prevent the war of 1812, brought about as English writers desire us to believe by the intrigues of Napoleon, and while it was in progress visited Europe for the purpose of securing the mediation of Russia to bring it to a close. He was the chief personage in negotiating the treaty of Ghent. In 1816 he was appointed Minister to France which place he held till 1823. He was considered at Paris one of the most eminent members of the diplomatic body. He was a favorite of Lewis Eighteenth, and numbered among his friends many of the most eminent statesmen, scientists and literary personages of the time. In the list were Madame de Stael, then living at Geneva, Humboldt, Laplace, Lafayette, the Duke de Broglie, and Lord and Lady Ashburton. Madame de Stael died while he was in Paris. His salary as American Minister was small, but from his private means he maintained a handsome establishment, and gathered around him a brilliant coterie. It is not easy to comprehend how so rank a Republican as Gallatin, most of whose life had been passed in the backwoods west of the Alleghanies, should have been found so congenial to the aristocratic Court of Louis Eighteenth and been received on such terms of social intimacy by the King himself. The signs of irritation occasionally manifested toward America and Americans at that period never had personal relation to him. Gilman in his biography, speaking of the relations of the American Minister to the King, says that Louis the Eighteenth was a Bourbon to the ends of his fingers. He had the *bonhomie* dashed with malice that characterized the race. The good-natured satire which was the acquired tone of the French society of the period was native to Gallatin. He was kindly and familiarly received at Court and at the *petits soupers* which were the delight of the epicurean King where His Majesty on more than one occasion shelled the crawfish for the little daughter of the republican minister. A compliment was once paid to Gallatin's French to which the King assented, but added "But I believe my English is better than yours." He had established his reputation as a financier before going to Europe. His success in negotiating the treaty of Ghent placed him on a level with the best European diplomatists. His genius was universally recognized. Sismondi, the historian, praised him. Madame de Stael expressed the warmest admiration for his abilities. He was the intimate friend of Alexander Baring, whose name must be added to the list of those already mentioned. After being relieved of his office he made a tour of Europe before returning to America. He was succeeded by Richard Rush who was indebted to him for his advancement.

James Fennimore Cooper.

In 1832 James Fennimore Cooper visited Europe and remained three years spending a considerable portion of the time at Paris. It was a period of political disturbance. Louis

Philippe had just come to the throne, on which he felt so insecure that it seemed possible he might be overthrown at any moment and again find himself in exile. The novelist was already known to French readers. All of his tales thus far had been translated and published by Galignani. His reminiscences of his tour were printed some years later and like all books of European travel of fifty years ago are curious by way of contrast with what is written by *blasé* tourists in these days of rapid communication for better informed and therefore less interested readers. His reception in aristocratic circles was cordial. Lafayette was living alone in the rue d'Anjou his family being in the country. Cooper used to come informally at the dinner hour, being always sure of finding Lafayette alone and accessible. He occupied a small apartment of three or four rooms, and dined from a table the size of an American washstand so small that it could be covered with a napkin. He spoke with frankness of the Americans he had known. He attributed the execution of Louis Sixteenth to the bad advice given him by Gouverneur Morris, whom he regarded as honest in motive but rash in counsel, and too aristocratic in his sympathies. Of his own, and of his family's obligations to Morris he spoke with gratitude, though it was plain that he could not understand why an American statesman educated in the school of the American Revolution could not agree with the sentiments entertained by the Girondists and the circle which was wont to gather at Madame de Tesse's. It happened about this time that Mr. M'Lane came over from London and as Lafayette was to present him to the King, Cooper was asked to be one of the party. He describes Louis Philippe as speaking English correctly but with a marked accent. He shook hands with his American visitors who were afterwards presented to the Queen and the princesses. The Queen did not extend her royal hand to be shaken. He describes her as a thin graceful woman who might have been prettier in her youth. Princess Adelaide the King's sister had no beauty left except sweetness of expression. The young princesses were simply dressed and without ornament. Lafayette was not satisfied with the public reception accorded to his American friends, and before they left arranged for another in one of the smaller salons. To this the King came with evident reluctance saying a few words to Mr. M'Lane and nothing to the novelist who stood in the background. All the Americans present at the reception were invited to dinner soon afterwards. Though Lafayette was treated with a certain ceremonial courtesy at court it was apparent to the writer that the King did not regard him with favor. Cooper wrote in detail about Paris, which was not then the beautiful city it has since become, and of monuments which interested him as they must interest every intelligent traveller.

Notes and Criticism. The Tuileries did not please him architecturally. He said of French manners what was usual to American travellers of the period. They were in his opinion the finest in the world though necessarily artificial. The time had long passed when French art, society, and politics were regarded through the discolored medium of English prejudice. Feeling toward the United States was not universally favorable though on the whole cordial. Living he found to be dearer in Paris than in America. All articles of table luxury unless of French fabrication cost more than in New York. Clothing was much cheaper though neither the English nor the French were habitually as well dressed as the Americans, by which he merely meant to say that the garments of his countrymen were of better material and better made though not so elegant in fashion. It is often said now of the dress of an American gentleman that it is not only as elegant in form as can be seen in Europe but it is far superior to the clothing seen abroad in material and in the qualities that tend to render it durable. American ladies may be pleased to know that in Cooper's opinion his countrywomen more than fifty years ago were more graceful and danced better than English women, and were even then distinguished for smaller hands and

feet than European ladies in general. The contrary idea prevailed
in Europe where it was thought that everything in America even
the human extremities had a certain immensity. He illustrated
this by an anecdote. When in Switzerland he bought twelve or
fifteen rings to distribute among a like number of his countrywomen who happened to be at Vevay. All but three had to be
made smaller and when he presented them he was laughed out of
countenance. The novelist was a man of irritable temper and his
stay in Europe was not without personal disagreements. He
excited the ire of Hazlitt, who had previously studied art in Paris.
He saw him at a social gathering talking with Lafayette and
thinking him an American asked who he was. Lafayette told
him, and offered an introduction, which Cooper, in accordance
with some fixed rule by which he was governed, declined. Hazlitt
afterwards wrote of him as screwing his face up in a corner in his
effort to be noticed and going about describing himself as the
"American Walter Scott." Cooper attributes this display of ill-
nature to the lack of eagerness he manifested in making Hazlitt's
acquaintance. He also had personal difference with some one at
Galignani's whom he thought Mr. Galignani himself, but who it
afterwards appeared was only an employé. The attention he
received from persons in every class of society more than com-
pensated for the slights real and imagined which he received.
The "Bravo" was written while he was abroad. Several of its
most exciting situations were illustrated by French artists at the
Salon of 1833. When he returned from Switzerland he visited
Lafayette at his chateau, and was received with the greatest
warmth by the entire family. The following extract from a letter
of Lafayette refers to Gouverneur Morris:

I have read the memoirs of a distinguished statesman to whose memory I am
bound by a seal of early friendship and an affectionate gratitude for the great
services he rendered in the most dangerous times to my wife and children. Yet
I cannot deny that his communications with the royal family representing me as
an ultra-democrat and republican even for the meridian of the United States
were among the numerous causes which encouraged them in their opposition to
my advice and to public opinion. For my part I have in the course of a long
life ever experienced that distance instead of relaxing does enliven and brace my
sentiments of American pride.

General Lewis Cass. The ministry of General Cass was memorable for many reasons. Louis Philippe, the Citizen King, had passed his years of exile in the United States where he had learned to understand and to appreciate Americans. He spoke English it may almost be said like a native. Washington was his ideal hero. His reign was remarkable fo courtesies shown by him and his court to the Americans then living in Paris, who were not numerous, and to American travellers of distinction who visited France. General Cass had participated in the war of 1812, and having been disgusted with the surrender of Fort Dearborn, he remained all his life an anglophobe which did not render him less acceptable to the French, whose traditional dislike for England was perennial and whose memories of Waterloo were still green. His wife was a refined and charming woman of simple domestic habits, and he had several daughters, who enlivened the handsome entertainments which he gave in the spacious ministerial residence in the Avenue Matignon. Having a considerable private income he was not circumscribed in his expenditure. Hence his hospitality assumed a form not covenient to later ministers whose means have been more limited. It seems anomalous that in the early days of the republic, when it was poor and struggling, its representatives assumed a mode of life in Paris and lived among surroundings that were not entirely consistent with the poverty of the country that sent them, or with the abstract idea of republican simplicity. Franklin maintained his establishment at Passy on a liberal scale, receiving as familiar guests at his table a large circle of the most notable men of France. Jefferson lived with great elegance in his house in the Cul-de-sac Têtebout. The fine ladies and gentlemen who still fluttered like moths about the candle, in the gay life of Paris during the gloomy days that served as vestibule to the Terror, flocked to Mr. Morris's elegant mansion in the Rue de la Planche, some to pay him social homage others to seek assistance. There were potent reasons during the first fifty years of the national existence of the American republic why it should make some degree of social display in foreign countries. It was weak and needed to assert itself by every legitimate means. This will serve as explanation, if explanation is needed, of the endeavor made by the early American ministers to accommodate themselves to the life about them. The country was unknown. Push was needed, the quality that has since made the name of the United States synonymous with enterprise. The Americans as a nation are no longer unknown. They still assert themselves, though not by installing their ministers and consuls in palaces after the manner of Great Britain and furnishing them with unlimited means to maintain by social display the prestige of the nation. Yet allowing all the tribute necessary to republican simplicity it remains an open question whether the United States superbly rich in reality, and having undeveloped resources of inconceivable value, might not sometimes treat more liberally its foreign branch of the civil service without incurring the reproach of wastefulness. Mr. Cass was the last of the social barons of the diplomatic service of the United States in France, the last but one to occupy an entire building, or residence, for his family and the business of the Legation.

Thorn and Corbin. Though American residents were not numerous in Paris during the reign of Louis Philippe, there were two who attained social eminence and have not since been forgotten. One of these was Colonel Thorn, the other Francis P. Corbin. Colonel Thorn had been in the marine service of the United States where he had acquired an experience that afterwards proved to him of great value. He was a man of handsome person and prepossessing manners. While still young he married clandestinely the daughter of an Englishman of enormous wealth, who though he consented to live separately in the same house with his son-in-law, and furnished him with sufficient means to maintain a handsome establishment refused to be reconciled to him to the end of his days. This lack of recognition appears to have been attended with bitterness of feeling on one side only. On one occasion a fire occurred in the dead of night. Colonel Thorn at considerable danger to his own life picked up his aged and helpless relative and carried him out of the house without the subject of the gallant act being even aware of the identity of his preserver. He did not even relent when informed that his own son-in-law had risked his life to save him. There are those like " Cleveland " in Scott's romance, " The Pirate," who can forgive injuries more readily than benefits. In due time children were born and grew up in the Thorn household. The eldest son became the favorite of his grandfather who stipulated in his will that the young man should be sent to Oxford to be educated. The unrelenting sire was gathered to his fathers while the young man was at the university, and the latter was not long afterwards killed by a fall from his horse while hunting. Colonel Thorn became his son's heir and came to Paris to spend his income which amounted to a hundred thousand dollars a year a much larger sum in those days than now. He spent it all and something more. His style of living was magnificent. His turnouts were the finest in France the royal equipages of the King not excepted. He entertained the nobility at his house in Paris, and at the chateau which he leased in Normandy he had always about him as numerous a company of guests as can be found at the country-seat of an English nobleman. There his rural hospitality was on almost as lavish a scale as that of the earls and barons of the times of Queen Elizabeth. His public display sometimes bordered on eccentricity. His turnout of the afternoon was entirely distinct from that of the morning. His horses had other trappings, and his carriage other armorial bearings. The livery of his servants including the buttons was of quite another color and pattern. This was about the period when that social explorer, Mrs. Trollope, found such a bewildering lack of refinement in the western wilds of the United States. She observed Colonel Thorn in Paris and made his turnouts the subject of some strictures conceived in the spirit of her books of American travel. Though leading an extravagant life Colonel Thorn seems to have had the esteem of the higher classes in France. It is quite certain that he had their society

4

whenever he desired it which was often. After having lived a
quarter of a century in France, and having somewhat diminished
his colossal fortune by his expenditure, Colonel Thorn returned to
New York where he built and occupied a large brown-stone front
house near Fourteenth street. Here he died a few years later. He
left a large family of children among whom was divided the large
fortune which had come into his possession in such a romantic
manner. Many years after his death one of his grandsons in a fit
of intoxication fell down an area and was so badly injured that he
was taken to a hospital in an adjacent street where he died. This
hospital chanced to be the building that had served as the Thorn
mansion in its better days.

Turn, Fortune, turn thy wheel and lower the proud.

Mr. Corbin was a Virginian. He had married a rich Philadelphia heiress, and was considered a man of great fortune. He
came to Paris before 1830 and made it his home till he died
some fifty years later. He was a man of cultivated tastes and
elegant manners, and conspicuous in the best society of the city.
One of his daughters married Viscount de Dampierre the other
the Duke de Montmort.

Siege and Commune. The last official dinner given at the
Tuileries by Napoleon Third was in
honor of the United States Minister and
Mrs. Washburne. There were numerous guests and the repast was
served in the usual sumptuous style of the Imperial household.
The trouble with Germany was approaching a crisis and a feeling
of uneasiness pervaded the Court and official circles. The
Emperor was courteous to the guests of the occasion, and made
inquiries of the Minister in regard to business between the two
countries and the health of the President. He said that he
intended to send as minister to the United States M. Prevost-
Paradol, a clever man but unskilled in diplomacy, which called
forth the remark from Mr. Washburne that considering the cordial
relations of the two countries this was a matter of minor import-

ance. It was the last time that the Minister saw the Emperor, as this meeting was on the seventh of June and war being soon afterwards declared he left for the front to command the army in person. In the important events that followed Sedan, the siege of Paris and the brief rule of the Commune, Mr. Washburne as representative of the United States was destined to play an important part. He saw the Empress once after the first serious defeat of the French armies. This visit was rendered necessary by the reception of a note from Washington which official etiquette required him to present in person. The Empress having left St. Cloud sent him a word that she would receive him at the Tuileries. He described the meeting in one of the articles published in *Scribner's Magazine.* After being formally admitted and having delivered his message the Empress, who had evidently passed a sleepless night, alluded to the bad news that had been received and began to discuss its probable effect on the French people. He suggested that the defeat might not have been so disastrous as had been reported and spoke of the first battle of Bull Run which only stimulated the Americans to greater effort. She replied that she only wished the French resembled the Americans in this respect, but she feared they would become discouraged and give up the contest. Soon after this the cares of office began to be heaped on Mr. Washburne. The German Government requested the United States to look after the safety of its citizens in Paris who when the war began numbered over thirty thousand. After Sedan Madame McMahon came to him to get a pass for her husband who had been wounded. During the siege he was the only representative of a foreign government in Paris, and as such exercised a paternal care over what seemed to him "half the nationalities of the earth." There was a constant demand for passports, there being no other authority within the city able to issue them. Most of the Americans had gone before the siege began, but a large delegation of those remaining consisting of forty-eight men, women and children left in carriages by the Creteil gate some time after the investment was completed. They were accompanied by a sufficient number of English and Russians having the passes of the American Minister to swell the cortege to two hundred. Enough remained to make a colony of respectable size and these bore the dangers and deprivations of the siege with cheerfulness and courage, suffering sometimes from cold, eating the strange kinds of food to which long-besieged populations find themselves reduced, and finding their chief distraction in deeds of benevolence.

The Legation and Its Work.

It was the second time in the history of Paris that an American minister found himself the only foreign representative remaining in the city. These two periods were the most turbulent of the many stormy epochs through which it has passed and the danger from a lawless and not easily controlled portion of the population was not to be disregarded. Nathan Sheppard says in his "Shut up in Paris" that there were the best reasons for believing that the Legation was at one time in danger of a hostile manifestation, the advisability of ordering the entire Anglo-Saxon population out of the city being seriously debated in the revolutionary circles of the Belleville quarter. The personnel of the United States Legation during the siege comprised the Minister, Honorable E. B. Washburne, his private secretary, Albert Lee Ward, and Colonel Wickham Hoffman, Secretary of Legation. Colonel Hoffman, was acting as *Chargé d'Affaires* when the Legation at the request of the North German Confederation took the subjects of the Confederation under its protection, Mr. Washburne being ill at Carlsbad. The Minister returned to his post two or three days later. The Olivier Government gave permission to German subjects to remain in France so long as their conduct gave no legitimate ground for complaint, and forbade the departure of Prussians liable to military duty. The Palikao Government to protect itself and to save the Germans from an unreasonable populace ordered them all to leave the country. Mr. Washburne's remonstrances were unavailing, and he found himself obliged to superintend the departure of over thirty thousand German subjects which was not accomplished without overcoming apparently insurmountable difficulties and the occurrence of personal scenes calculated by their pathos to move the stoniest nature to compassion. The number of women and children unable to leave was two thousand three hundred. Some of these were arrested and thus made safe from personal danger. Some were placed in Catholic and Protestant orphan asylums where their board was paid by Mr. Washburne, and they were regularly visited by messengers from the Legation. The lower story of the Legation building was fitted up for the remainder and they were fed with such food as could be found in the city during this destitute period. It was not toward the Germans alone that the American Minister acted the part of the Good Samaritan. The English who remained in Paris united in testifying their gratitude for the substantial service rendered by him and others attached to the Legation which became such a resort of persons asking aid and seeking news as to fairly encumber the place and render the transaction of business difficult. The Legation proved itself of great use to Frenchmen and the French authorities. All official communications passed through its hands and were carefully copied by its employés. So were the numberless personals in the *Times* which were sent to the Paris papers for publication. The Legation acted the part of postmaster to Paris. Letters from the outside world necessarily came through the "American bag," a receptacle which had its secret diplomatic history. It was in charge of Mr. Benjamin Moran, who fulfilled his duties faithfully though often exposed to rare perils without and within the hostile lines arising from the fear of each of the armies that it might be used as a means of *espionnage* or to further the intrigues of the other. The United States Consul-General at the time was John Meredith Read whose conduct was in its generosity and spirit of self-devotion perfectly in keeping with that of the Legation. Of Mr. Washburne it may be said in general terms that the country was happily represented for so critical a period. Without being a man of the highest culture he had a certain kindness of nature and an extensive political experience acquired during an active and trying period of American history that fitted him admirably for the task which fell to his lot so unexpectedly. The impulses of a generous nature were aided always by a judicious promptness of action. The political training which our first ministers to France had received during the revolutionary war and the first years of the republic had their counterpart in his own similar experience during the war of the Rebellion.

Minister and Commune. When the Government retired to Versailles Mr. Washburne took a small office in a side street in that city but returned every night to Paris. His passing back and forth was with slight interruption from the Communards. The favors he asked from persons in authority were always granted though not in every case cordially. When Archbishop Darboy was arrested and imprisoned, at the request of the Pope's Nuncio he visited General Cluseret, Minister of War, and frankly told him that the incarceration of the archbishop on the pretence of holding him as a hostage was an outrage, and that the Commune should in its interest release him. Cluseret agreed but said that the case did not come within his province, and that if he interfered he should only make the condition of the prisoner worse. The Minister expressed a desire to visit the prisoner, but this could not be accomplished without application to Raoul Rigault, Procureur of the Commune. Permission was obtained through the General who accompanied the Minister to the Prefecture of Police and personally asked Rigault for it. It was in the power of the visitor only to pay his compliments and offer his sincere sympathies. A second permit was obtained from Rigault with great difficulty. It gave permission to " Citizen Washburne " to visit the " prisoner Darboy." He was not admitted to the Archbishop's cell, but conferred with him in the presence of the guard. The removal of the prisoner from the Mazas prison to that of La Roquette prevented a third call upon him. The Archbishop with Abbé Duguerry, President Bonjean and the other hostages were shortly afterwards executed in the court of La Roquette. Mr. Washburne's course in this matter and the siege during the entire rule of the Commune was brave, humane, and sensible, and won the encomiums of all persons of all nations who had the opportunity of observing his action.

Flight of the Empress. The escape of the Empress from Paris after the fall of the Empire forms one of the most romantic episodes of the period. She knew very well of what material the baser part of the Paris population was made and what crimes it was capable of when freed from restraint. She had no desire that her name should be coupled in history with that of the hapless Marie Antoinette. Still the popular feeling had been wrought up to the highest pitch and the danger was close at hand before she deemed it necessary to make efforts to escape. Her last official interview with Count Palikao was on Sunday, September fourth, when she was informed that the Assembly had been driven from the Chamber by the mob who had gone to the Hotel-de-Ville with the Extreme Left to proclaim the Republic with General Trochu as the civil and military head of it. She declined the offer of the Count to endeavor to rally the troops and make a last stand for the Empire. It was late in the afternoon, and a crowd of evil aspect had gathered about the Tuileries whose flag had been hauled down by some thoughtful person to give the impression that the Empress had already gone. Their cries could be distinctly heard without and the ring of their arms as they penetrated further into the building, and began mounting the staircase. There were with her at the moment besides some members of her household Prince Metternich, M. Nigra, and her friend Madame Le Breton sister of General Bourbaki. It was impossible to reach the street by way of the courtyard the Place du Carrousel being full of people therefore the party decided to traverse the entire length of the Louvre and go out at the opposite end into the Place St. Germain-Auxerrois named from the church which fronts one side of it and is famous for having been the first to sound the tocsin on the night of St. Bartholomew. The palace is of great length and this exit being fully half a mile from the Tuileries no one would have thought of looking for the imperial fugitive here even if it had been known that she was trying to escape. Emerging into the colonnade and looking along the short passage which is separated from the gardens on either side by a tall railing they saw that the street was full of people crying "Déchéance ! " " Vive la République ! " Still an angry mob was on all sides of them and they could not pause. None of the party.who had left the Tuileries remained but the two ladies and the two foreign Ministers. The ladies were thinly veiled, and some person who tradition says was either a *gamin* or a woman of the people cried out "The Empress ! " No one heeded, and before any further attention had been attracted to them they had entered a close fiacre which happened to be standing near and giving a fictitious address were driven out of sight. It is useless now to speculate on what might have been the fate of the Empress had she fallen into the hands of those merciless hags descendants of the *tricotteuses* who daily surrounded the guillotine during the Revolution and who a few months later won distinction as the *pétróleuses* of the Commune.

A Port of Refuge. In passing through the Boulevard Haussmann the ladies found that in their haste to leave the place they had neglected to provide themselves with money and now had but three francs between them. They dismounted at once lest the fare should exceed their means and cause trouble, and pursued their way to the residence of Dr. Evans in the Avenue du Bois de Boulogne. Dr. Evans was naturally surprised to see his guests of whose danger he had not been made aware, but he received them .cordially and loyally and took such action as the emergency required. Mrs. Evans was at Deauville wither he resolved to conduct the ladies in a carriage the moment he found that he could pass the barriers in safety. After having sufficiently reconnoitred he set out in his own carriage the ladies being suitably disguised and a gentleman associated with him in a business capacity accompanying the party in the guise of a footman. Being personally well known he succeeded in passing the limits of the city without exciting suspicion and continued his course to St. Germain and Mantes where he stopped at a hotel, sent his own carriage and horses back to Paris and hired another to continue his journey. This method of procedure was taken several times before reaching Deauville the entire distance having been travelled without the slightest accident or arousing the faintest suspicion of the identity of the Empress. There were two yachts in the harbor. The owner of the largest was absent so they went to the other, the *Gazelle*, which was owned by Sir John Burgoyne. They told their story and asked him to take them across to England. He hesitated at first fearing some international complication, but finally consented requesting only that the Empress should come on board just before sailing in order not to attract the attention of the townspeople among whom strange rumors were already afloat. The precaution proved necessary for the vessel received some visitors evidently bent on finding out whether there were others on her besides the owner and his crew. The Empress, Madame Le Breton and Dr. Evans came on board at the appointed moment and the *Gazelle* got safely out of Deauville harbor and into one of the most fearful storms that had visited the Channel for many years. She was a tiny vessel and it was at one time feared that she must inevitably go to the bottom, but she rode out the tempest and on the eighth of September entered the harbor of Ryde in safety. The party went first to Brighton and then to Hastings where the Empress rejoined the Prince Imperial. The Empress being homeless, and without a friend in England it became necessary for Dr. Evans to find for her some suitable residence. After diligent search Camden House at Chiselhurst was leased on reasonable terms. Dr. Evans afterwards visited the Emperor in his German prison and spent some weeks in endeavoring to alleviate the condition of the three-hundred thousand French soldiers held in Germany as prisoners of war. In this work he had the cordial co-operation of the Empress Augusta to whom he made a hasty visit at Berlin after bidding the Empress Eugénie farewell at Chiselhurst.

The American Ambulance.

The American ambulance system had been brought during the war of the Rebellion to a degree of perfection unknown in Europe. The French had been made partially familiar with its workings by the efforts of Dr. Evans who had published several works on the subject or on sanitary matters closely allied thereto, and had, by the intelligent assistance of Dr. E. A. Crane who visited the United States for the purpose, made an admirable collection of inventions and appliances for ameliorating the condition of wounded soldiers which formed one of the most interesting features of the Paris Universal Exposition of 1867. It remained however for the Americans in Paris during the siege to illustrate in a practical manner the workings of the American ambulance system and to show at the same time the native tendency of the American character towards deeds of benevolence. When the Franco-Prussian war began, the material which had formed the exhibit at the Exposition was got in order by Dr. Evans and made ready in all essential details for efficient work at the front. Events succeeded one another with such rapidity that it was unable to leave Paris. A few days after Sedan the German army moving with incredible celerity was at the city gates and the siege commenced. Fate had decided that the noble mission of the ambulance should be performed in the heart of Paris and not on the eastern frontier or on German soil. Dr. Evans being absent the superintendence of the work devolved on his lieutenant Dr. Crane who was fitted for it by temperament and long experience as an army surgeon and officer of the United States Sanitary Commission during the civil war. The place selected for pitching the hospital tents was in the broadest part of the Avenue de l'Impératrice now the Avenue du Bois de

Boulogne. Winter was at hand and the manner of heating them had to be decided a matter of considerable difficulty as the area was almost that of a small country town. The problem was solved by conducting the heat by means of trenches through the wards and so successfully that an even and sufficient temperature was maintained during one of the most rigorous winters experienced in the latitude for many years. The hospital contained two hundred beds none of which were ever unoccupied. The field service was performed by ten or twelve ambulance wagons made according to the most recent models and in charge of picked men. Nothing was wanting that could render the service humane and effective either in field or hospital. The chief personnel of the ambulance comprised beside Dr. Crane, Rev. W. O. Lamson, Albert Lee Ward, Dr. John Swinburne, surgeon, and Dr. W. E. Johnston. All were Americans. The volunteer aids comprised twenty-three gentlemen and fourteen ladies who worked assiduously early and late. Mr. Sheppard says of the ambulance and its work, " It was one of the most conspicuous features of the siege. Its neat and tasteful grounds, its ample and well-ventilated hospital tents, and above all the skill and fidelity of Surgeon Swinburne and the energy of his fellow-workers on the field and at the bedside must ever be remembered in Paris with gratitude and delight." Still more to the point because coming from an alien and therefore unprejudiced source is the testimony of. Thomas Gibson Bowles correspondent of the London *Post* who remained in Paris during the siege. The extract is from his book published shortly afterwards " The Defense of Paris " :

Of all the ambulances the American is the only one that does its work in a business like manner and it has in its tents a kind of family party which is the most amusing sight to an unattached Englishman. Fancy a grizzly-bearded, sure-handed surgeon working for pure philanthrophy with a heart as soft as his language is strong, a spruce Quakeress scandalized at the slightest impropriety, two ladies of the opera, an extremely evangelical person believing in the efficacy of texts printed in French, a number of bankers and idle young men believing in nothing at all, a stray Englishman or two, and finally a rich lady of color who has left her luxury in order to perform the most menial offices for the wounded and to be snubbed by the rest of the ambulance, a truly adorable woman whose utter self-abnegation and devotion should win her a high seat at that place where there is no respect for persons. They are all littered down together in an open piece of ground which they have covered with tents whence they issue always first on the field of battle to snatch away the wounded. It rejoices one to see the workmanlike and yet tender care they give to the unhappy victims and the untiring way in which they devote themselves. There is my friend for instance who has sat up for the last two nights working like a horse till I am positively ashamed to look him in the face when I think that I am doing nothing at all for them.

The good work done by the ambulance was recognized in the most generous manner by the Thiers Government. Dr. Evans who had inaugurated the enterprise and who paid all the expenses afterwards was made Commander of the Legion of Honor and the order was conferred on sixteen of his auxiliaries. There were also numerous expressions of heartfelt gratitude on the part of the French press and people.

THE AMERICAN COLONY.

The Americans have not like the English formed colonies abroad for economical reasons, not that they scorn economy, but they do not find unless they exile themselves to country towns that living in Europe is much cheaper than it is at home. Their chief motive in leaving America has been first pleasure then health and the education of their children. The desire to be amused drew them to Rome when the Pope was a ruling sovereign in his States and his ecclesiastical court gave a peculiar brilliancy to the life of the Immortal City, and to Dresden when it was an independent monarchy and its King and Queen assumed the grand airs of royalty. The American Colony in London would long ago have acquired a much greater importance had the Queen of England sooner seen fit to doff her widow's weeds, and that of Paris would be much larger to-day were there still a Court at the Louvre maintained with royal or imperial splendor. Sumptuary laws not being in vogue in this enlightened era the rich American is free to go where he pleases and scatter his gold in a perfect shower of Danaë if it so likes him. He would not go abroad at all if he did not find something novel in the lands beyond the sea, if he could not make the acquaintance of men things and a society in sharp contrast with the life of his neighbors and the scenes among which he has been reared. His fondness for the gayety of a foreign Court does not imply a surrender of principle. He is not less an American because he has gone to a ball at the Tuileries, nor need it be supposed that he would prefer to see an autocrat in the chair of the President at Washington because he is gratified with the cordiality with which he is received by a King or Emperor. He, a sovereign and gentleman, coming from a country where all decent men have that distinction, meets the foreign potentate as a sovereign and gentleman ; only this and nothing more. The American is far from being a socialist. He is quite willing to believe that a European ruler is the peer of a citizen of the great Republic till his unworthiness of such honorable association has been proved. The United States is governed by the high average intelligence and sterling good sense of the mass of the people. Such social conditions exist in no other country. Few thoughtful Americans believe that every country in Europe is prepared by a similar enlightenment of its people to take upon itself the responsibility of similar institutions. They even sometimes permit themselves to think that Kings and Emperors have their place in the providential scheme of the world's government, an additional reason why they should not reject their society. There are Americans living in Paris, constituting probably only a minority of the Colony, who however much they may wish to see France a great and prosperous republic, do not think that public sentiment is yet ripe for that result. This does not mean that their own preference for the republican form of government has undergone any change whatever. New England spinsters whose thin blood has trickled down in a constantly attenuating stream from one of Cromwell's troopers through a long line of pious Puritan ancestry have been known to lament what they regarded as the usurpation of Italy in taking Rome as its capital and dispossessing the Pope. This does not signify that the descendants of the Puritans are trying to seek shelter in the bosom of that church from which they have been separated since Henry the Eighth. This is a brief summary of the reasons why Americans did not in the times of such true republican statesmen as Franklin, Jefferson and Morris, and do not now feel obliged to look upon royalty with abhorence or think that they deny their principles in mingling with the society about a foreign monarch or spending a considerable part of their lives at a foreign capital. There may be Americans infatuated with a titled aristocracy or smitten with blind admiration for the life of royal courts, but they are exceptional and excite ridicule. They serve only to emphasize the argument and prove the rule.

The Colonial Character. The permanent American Colony is nearly all composed of persons whose labor is that of the lilies of the field. This must not be regarded as their fault. Some were born to fortunes, others achieved them. There are in the list a goodly number of artists some of whom have inherited riches and added to it by their talent while others have become independent by the exercise of their profession alone. There are a few journalists working on newspapers printed in Paris in the English language, and a greater number acting as foreign correspondents for American daily papers. The number of Americans in Paris engaged in commerce is not large. Some of these represent large American houses while others have manufactures or shops of their own. Nearly all are relatively prosperous. It may be said respecting the distribution of wealth in the colony that enormous fortunes are not the rule. Quite a number are millionaires in dollars. A majority, perhaps, are millionaires in francs, while a notable proportion are in the financial condition of that easily contented scriptural character who prayed that he might neither be burdened with riches or oppressed by poverty. The number of Americans who receive salaries as clerks laborers or menials is small. In this respect the difference between the English and the American colony is remarkable. Wealthy Englishmen do not live abroad in considerable numbers unless engaged in banking or in commerce. The middle classes go where rents are low and food cheap as to German cities, Swiss towns, or in winter to deserted watering places like Ostend. The English in Paris are engaged in trade, or as laborers, hostlers, or domestics. They number eight or ten thousand. A wealthy English resident of Paris is a rare exception to the rule. England is so near that her rich people can come and go as they please. Germans, Italians, Swiss and Belgians who form an important element of the Paris population are chiefly engaged in petty trade or occupied in the various avenues of labor. There are numerous Mexican, Central American and South American nabobs but they do not form a colony. It is evident from this statement of facts that the relations of the Americans to Paris are different from those of any other nation. Though numerically so small they possess a greater aggregate of wealth than the subjects, if not of all, certainly. than those of any two or three European nations combined. This wealth inures to the benefit of Paris and its citizens in proportion. As the United States is the best customer that France and Paris have abroad so the American colony is the best customer that Paris has at home. When France has been in trouble the Americans have always turned the warmest side of their character toward her. The Americans at home and the American Colony in Paris have given freely of their substance. The story of the American ambulance has already been told. During the Franco-Prussian war Americans at home and abroad gave more to alleviate the suffering caused by it than the entire amount contributed by the French people and as much as all the rest of Europe. It is nothing to boast of, but it will do no harm to remember it when the French accuse the Americans of ingratitude because they did not come to their aid with a fleet and army after their defeat at Sedan. They have not only given their money but their heart with it.

Not Gregarious. It is sometimes alleged against the American colony that it is not sufficiently gregarious. It may be true that a cloud sometimes intercepts the sunshine of colonial life, but there are reasons, and the evil is magnified by malicious persons. Colonies are proverbially inharmonious. There are inherent defects in that mode of existence. Take the English colonies in the Far East as an example. When a little knot of Englishmen find themselves alone together in some remote spot, the island of Formosa, for instance, the first task they set themselves is a social one, namely to separate the sheep from the goats. For a country with a theory of constitutional liberty and equality only equalled by that of one other nation, the aristocratic idea is inbred in Englishmen in a manner that is as incomprehensible as it is ineradicable. Though the colony may not number more than twenty-five persons the wholesale merchant cannot sit down with the retail dealer because the latter is of an inferior class and he would be defiled, neither can the customs official nor the commercial employé of a superior grade meet in any circle on terms of equality the official or employé of the grade below him without contamination. But this is not all. It is but the beginning of discord. Without obvious reason the hand of every man is against his neighbor and there are speedily developed nearly as many cliques in the little world as there are individuals. The bitterness is increased by the fact that as on shipboard the colonists cannot escape daily contact with one another. They must live together and fight it out on that line till death comes to their relief or some members of the colony are transferred to other posts. This is an extreme instance. Colonies are everywhere much the same though those of England develop the special symptoms with greatest virulence. Matters have never reached this crisis in the American colony in Paris. Compared with the intense personal bitterness engendered among Englishmen by colonial friction the feeling of Americans in Paris towards one another is that of tender fraternal affection. It is not strange that there should be a difference of opinion among them. The idea of the American national character is unity in variety. The country is large. It is composed of rival sections and of states having an individual character. Americans coming to Paris do not necessarily have common sympathies, that of country excepted, while they do to a certain extent have sectional prejudices such as exist in much smaller countries. The Frenchmen of the north for instance look at their countrymen of the south as in some sort inferior beings. No matter from what part of their country Americans come they never forget the national theory of equality, and if there are personal dislikes they are rarely on the ground of alleged inferiority. But intimate association is not necessary among these sybaritic exiles beyond a certain number of intimate friends. They have not all come to Paris with the same motive. The French capital having all that is necessary for human diversion within itself the society of one's countrymen is not found necessary for the first few years of residence. People naturally segregate into knots by a sort of chemical affinity of home association, that is those from Boston first seek to know those from Boston, those from Philadelphia those from Philadelphia and persons from the Southern States incline towards those associates that come from their own section. There is nothing to complain of in this. Nothing can be more natural, and no further explanation is needed respecting the existence of cliques. When these coteries go beyond these natural limits and lapse into undignified abuse of one another their conduct becomes reprehensible. Fortunately this is rare in the American colony. With some exceptions which must be considered as merely individual they bear and forbear, live and let live quite as reasonably and as amicably as any set of people so situated. Paris is large and they need not if they do not desire it be for ever brushing one another's garments as on shipboard or in a small Oriental settlement. A United States Minister can do much to heal the wounded vanity of his compatriots and level the social mole-hills that sometimes seem to form impassable barriers between different coteries. Most of those who have represented the country in Paris if they have been men of family and socially inclined have succeeded fairly well in this respect and during their tenure of office harmony has prevailed and dividing lines between cliques and coteries have almost disappeared. There have been others who perhaps have meant equally well, but either from maladroitness, or from weakly permitting themselves to be drawn this way or that by interested persons or by their personal preferences have increased rather than diminished the causes of discord. The remedy for a disease that is far from having reached its acute stages is not in attempting to suppress coteries that must always exist in a city where the distances are magnificent and where the differences of origin are so marked, but in foregoing prejudices, in oftener drawing the mantle of charity over individual failings and in substituting for envenómed personal speech a silence that is more than golden, is, indeed, refined gold itself.

Society During the Empire. As soon as Napoleon Third found himself established on the Imperial throne and beyond the reach of immediate danger he set himself to work to satisfy the wants and desires of the French people. There were the wealthy classes to be amused, the mercantile guilds who only wanted commerce stimulated, and the lower strata of society who must be kept out of mischief by being furnished with occupation. He proved himself equal to all these requirements especially to the first. He made his court the most brilliant in Europe, and had fluttering constantly about it the noble representatives of every European nation, and a large and constantly augmenting delegation of Americans many of whom became residents of Paris and formed a large and wealthy colony which received important accessions after the close of the Civil War. This colony was most numerous and most prosperous about the years 1868 and 1869, when in the absence of any authorized census its numbers may loosely be estimated at five thousand. The feelings of the court toward the members of the colony were cordial. The Emperor though an autocrat had always in him something of the leveling sentiment of democracy and the Empress who knew America well and spoke English perfectly was predisposed in their favor by having had as governess and companion an American lady who had been the wife of a Spanish grandee. Therefore there was always a liberal representation of Americans at the balls and receptions of the Tuileries. But as the colony increased in size the honors were more impartially divided. Where many American gentlemen were conspicuous for wealth, and many American ladies for beauty, there could not be the individual distinction enjoyed by certain eminent social personages in the time of Louis Philippe. There are many names that are still remembered, and some of these may be mentioned without seeming to separate them invidiously from others who had similar social prominence, such as Munroe, Rhodes, Richards, Evans, Beckwith, Wainwright, Storroch, Stewart, Selden, Chapin, Newbold and Reubell. Mrs. Wainwright was the wife of a well-known American merchant who entertained generously. Mrs. Storroch was a widow from Washington. Miss Rhodes married one of the sons of Mr. Corbin. Miss Chapin was one of the many young American ladies distinguished for her beauty. One of the Ministers during the early part of the Empire was Mr. Mason, a great admirer of the fair sex, but a widower and therefore entertaining little. The Empress was then at the height of her beauty and admired by every one, Mr. Mason among the rest. An incident regarding him has been greatly magnified. Being one evening at a ball or reception at the Tuileries he had the good fortune to be *en tête-à-tête* with the Empress longer than the time usually allotted to such interviews. He was seated beside her and in the blended charm of her beauty and her conversation so far forgot himself as to put his hand, not his arm, on the back of her chair so near that it unexpectedly, but quite gently, came in contact with her shoulder. Royal etiquette was certainly violated, but the offense was hardly so serious as if it had been committed by a younger and handsomer man. The Empress gave a start sufficiently marked to be noticed by a few critical and envious eyes, but showed no signs of anger and made no movement that attracted general attention. Being an Empress, her manners had necessarily the repose of the De Veres and something more. She had the good sense to understand and rate at its value a meaningless act that to a woman of narrower mind might have seemed like an extraordinary breach of decorum. The good feeling of both Emperor and Empress toward Americans continued till the last unaffected by the Maximilian incident which threatened at one moment to result in a war between France and the United States.

The Colony as It Is. Little remains to be be added to the comments already made on the American colony as it exists at present. It has its permanent and its floating elements, those who maintain establishments here and consider Paris as their only home and those who come annually and who are also in a sense colonists. It has its artists some of whom have lived here more than twenty years, and its art-students most of whom remain at least two years and often become permanent residents. James Gordon Bennett divides his time between Pau and his apartment in the Champs Élysées. Mrs. Lowery comes annually always taking rooms at the Hotel Bristol where the Vanderbilts, the Lorillards and other rich New York families also make their home when they are in Paris. It is the hotel invariably patronized by the Prince of Wales. Mrs. Henry Blake of Boston who comes often to Europe stops at a fashionable hotel in the rue Scribe. Mrs. Grant and her daughter who spend their winters at Cannes are so often at Paris as almost to be classed among the colonists. Among the people who entertain freely are Mrs. Bischoffsheim formerly Miss Payne of New York, Mrs. Parker who is noted for her kindness to struggling artists, the Robins, the Sorchans, Mrs. Moore, Mrs. Hawley of Chicago at whose salon are seen many of the French nobility, the Hoopers, Mrs. Gregory, Mrs. Jackson, Mrs. Dannat, Mrs. Haviland and Mrs. Gordon Pell. Mrs. Humphrey Moore, wife of the artist, numbers among her friends the Princess Mathilde and Madame Fortuny widow of the celebrated Spanish artist. Many of the Americans in Paris have been liberal patrons of art, and collectors of interesting relics of the past. Miss Bryant has a fine collection of bric-a-brac. The Stewart gallery of paintings is among the most noted in Paris while the Riggs collection of old armor is one of the most remarkable private museums of that kind in Europe. It is not, however, the intention to discuss too intimately the private affairs of the present members of the colony. The writing of even a sketch of contemporary history is exceedingly difficult and delicate especially when it relates to matters of a social nature, and to a class of persons not seeking the notoriety of the press. One thing about the Americans in Paris is the lingering attachment to their country that remains even among the oldest residents. Most of them, after years of experience, get tired of living abroad and return home to spend their declining years. Those who do not have formed family alliances or have other pressing reasons for prolonging their stay. One reason, why the colony has fallen off in numbers since the palmy days of the Empire is that it is not necessary now to come to Europe to be amused. The United States, in city and in country, has been absolutely transformed within thirty years. Its large cities have grown into great cosmopolitan centers of commercial activity, social life, and artistic feeling, having within themselves all that is necessary to make existence agreeable. All this does not furnish the attractions or supply the need of foreign travel. But it renders protracted residence in foreign countries less desirable. It has been discovered that life need not all be spent in gazing at the antiquities of Europe, in studying its museums of art, in attending its theaters or in listening to its music. Five or ten years suffice for that and the shortest of these two periods is enough to naturalize any good American as a citizen of the American Colony of Paris.

The Social List.   The list of Americans in Paris follows. A glance at it will show why the name has been changed from "American Colony in Paris" which was designed when the work was originally conceived. The present title affords the necessary elasticity. It is scarcely necessary to explain that the collection of the names has been an extremely arduous work resulting chiefly from reasons already given, namely, the subdivisions of the colony, and the slight knowledge they have or the absolute ignorance in which they often exist of one another. But even in its present form it will be found of unusual interest and great utility to the lady of fashion as well as to the general reader.

CALLING AND ADDRESS LIST.

Adams, S. Herbert ; 39 r l'Ambre
Aikens, Mrs. Andrew J. ; 7 ave Trocadéro
Ainsworth, Mrs. A. L. ; 10 r Philippe du Roule
Aberigh-Mackay, Rev. Dr. ; 19 ave l'Alma
Albertini, Mr. and Mrs. Diaz ; 25 ave Bois de Boulogne
    Reynolds, Mrs.
Alden, Mr. and Mrs. Robert Percy ; 5 r d'Antin
Alleman, Mrs. ; 35 r de Lubec
Allen, W. S. ; 7 ave Trocadéro
Allen, Thomas ; Écouen (Seine-et-Oise)
Alloo, Mr. and Mrs. L. J. ; 32 bd Haussmann
    Alloo, Miss
Anderson, David J. ; 7 r Tournon
Andrews, Mr. and Mrs. Clarence ; 22 r Galilée
Anthony, Professor Augustus M. ; 28 bd des Capucines
Appleton, Nathan ; 29 bd des Capucines
Armant, Mr. and Madame Raymond ; 32 r Rochefoucauld
    Armant, Mr. and Madame J. B.
Aron, Madame Joseph, Mondays ; Hotel Bedford
Arter, J. C. ; 35 r Cambon
Auffm-Ordt, Mr. and Mrs., Thursdays ; 10 ave Montaigne
Austin, Miss Eliza ; 1 r Lafitte
Austin, Willis R. ; 71 r Chaillot
Avard, Mr. and Mrs. ; 38 r Boursault
Aylmer, I. ; 4 r de Naples
Babcock, W. P. ; Barbizon

Bachelder, Mr. and Mrs. W. W. ; 26 r Pauquet
Bacon, Mr. and Mrs. Henry, Saturdays; 157 r Faubourg St Honoré
Bailly-Blanchard de Bourg; 36 r la Bruyère
    Bailly-Blanchard Arthur
Baker, Miss Ellen K. ; in America
Baldwin, Esther ; Hotel Balzac
Balch, Mrs. ; 28 cours de la Reine
    Balch, Miss
Bannvart, C. A. ; 11 *bis* r Blanche
Banuelos, Count and Countess ; 19 *bis* r Constantine
    Banuelos, Miss
    Banuelos, Miss A.
Barbey, Mr. and Mrs. Henry J. ; 118 ave Champs-Elysées
    Barbey, Misses
Barclay, Mr. and Mrs. Edmond, Wednesdays; 8 *bis* ave Percier
Barlow, J. N. ; 17 r du Départ
Barnard, Mr. and Mrs. C. Inman ; 20 r Constantinople
Barrett, Mde O. D., Fridays after 3 ; 59 ave Kléber
Bartholdi, Mr. and Mrs. ; 38 r Vavin
Batcheler, J. W.; 7 ave Victor Hugo
Bates, Mrs. I. C. ; 42 ave Champs-Elysées
Bates, Mrs. Samuel R. ; in America
    Bates, Miss
    Bates, Miss Alice
Beckman, Mrs. B. F. ; 1 r Pierre-Charron
Beer, Mrs. Bernhardt, Wednesdays ; ave de l'Alma
    Theriott, Louis
    Theriott, Miss
Bell, H. ; 30 r Faubourg St. Honoré
Benét, Lawrence ; address 21 r Royale
Berault, Mr. and Mrs. St. Maurice de
    Berault, Arthur, jr.
    Berault, Miss
Berg, John ; 27 r. la Rochefoucauld
Berhard, Dr. Harry ; 3 r Clément-Marot
    Berhard, Miss

Berhard, Miss Stella
Bernhardt, M. and Mde Alphonse ; 7 r Pierre-le-Grand
Bernstein, M. and Mde ; Fridays, 50 bd Courcelles
Beylard, Mrs. ; 66 ave d'Iéna
    Beylard, Misses
Biesel, Mr. and Mrs. Augustus ; 55 ave Victor-Hugo
Binda, Mr. and Mrs. Charles ; 11 r l'Echelle
Binder, Mr. and Mrs. George ; 6 ave McMahon
Bing, Dr. B. J. ; 26 r Cambon
Bird, Clarence A. ; 50 r Faubourg St. Denis
Bischoffsheim, Mr. and Mrs. Ferdinand ; 140 ave Champs-Elysées
Bispham, Mrs. Henry C. ; 6 ave Bois de Boulogne
Bissell, George ; 117 r Notre-Dame-des-Champs
Bixby, Miss Eula ; 9 ave McMahon
Blackall, Clara ; 48 r de Lille
Blackman, Mr. and Mrs. Walter, Fridays ; 28 r Pauquet
Blashfield, Mr. and Mrs. E. H. ; 164 bd Haussmann
Blood, Miss Olga ; 34 r Bassano
Blount, Mr. and Mrs. R. E. ; 89 ave Neuilly
Boggs, F. M. ; 11 bd Clichy
Boigne, Baron and Baroness ; 222 bd Pereire
    Boigne, Miss
Boit, Mr. and Mrs. Edward ; in America
Bonnemaison, Mr. and Mrs. Raoul ; 6 r Général Foy
Boreel, Madame ; 44 ave Marceau
Bos, Mr. and Mde du ; 3 r Christophe-Colomb
Bourdillon, Mr. and Mrs. ; 89 r Taitbout
    Melin, Mrs.
Bowen, Mr. and Mrs. J. Allison ; 44 ave Marceau
Boyden, Dwight F. ; 66 r de Seine
Boyland, Dr. G. Halstead ; 2 r Louis-le-Grand
Boyle, Mr. and Mrs. John J. ; 255, bd d'Enfer
Boyle, Miss Nellie D. ; 88 bd St. Michel
Bradford, Mrs. E. A. ; 12 r Kepler
Bridgman, Mr. and Mrs. F. A., Saturdays ; 144 bd Malesherbes
Bridgman, George B. ; 68 r Madame

Briere, Mr. and Mde Paul ; 3 r Laval
Bromley, F. B. ; 144 bd Malesherbes
Brooks, F.; 66 r de Seine
Brown, C. M. ; 63 r de Seine
Brown, James M. ; Hotel de Londres
    Brown, Miss
Brown, Mr. and Mrs. Neilson ; Hotel de l'Empire
Brown, Walter J. ; 10 r des Saints-Pères
Browne, Mr. and Mrs. Charles G. ; 10 r Trémoille
Brownell, Franklin ; 14 r Navarin
Brulatour, E. J. ; 5 place Malesherbes
Bryant, Miss Julia ; 30 r Galilée
Buckler, Dr. and Mrs. T. H. ; 2 r Presbourg
    Buckler, William
Bull, Miss Alice ; 17 quai d'Orsay
Bunker, Dennis M.; 16 bis r de la Gaîté
Burckhardt, Mr. and Mrs. S. E. ; 64 r de Courcelles
    Burckhardt, Miss
Burgess, Mr. and Mrs. Thomas; 115 ave Champs-Elysées
Burgess, Mr. and Mrs. William H., Thursdays ; 20 ave Kléber
Burke, Mr. and Mrs. Edmond ; 66 ave d'Iéna
Burnham, Mr. and Mrs. William C. ; 150 ave Champs-Elysées
Burns, Mrs. William ; 115 ave Champs-Elysées
Burnes, William Coleman ; 43 r Faubourg St. Honoré
Burnsley, J. M.; 119 ave St. Germain de Puteaux
Bush-Brown, H. R. ; 255 bd d'Enfer
Butler, H. R. ; 147 r Villiers
Butterfield, Henry J. ; 6 bis r Presbourg
    Butterfield, Louis
Cachard, Mr. and Mrs. Edward ; 18 ave Victor Hugo
    Cachard, Henry
    Cachard, Edward
Cahuzac, Hippolyte ; 30 ave Friedland
Caldwell, Leslie ; 31 bd Mont-Parnasse
Canonge, Mr. ; 70 ave d'Iéna
    Canonge, Miss

Camposelice, Duke and Duchess ; 27 ave Kléber
Carl, Katherine A.; 36 r Washington
Carriere, Jean ; 9 r Ecuries d'Artois
Carroll, Mr. and Mrs. John Lee ; 35 r François-Premier
    Lagrange, Baron and Baroness de
    Kergorlay, Count and Countess de
Carron, Mrs. James D.; 157 bd Malesherbes
Castro, Jules de ; 14 ave d'Eylau
Caubert, A.; 9 r de Grenelle
Cauchois, Mde E. L.; 9 r Gœthe
Chadwick, Mr. and Mrs. F. B.; Gres
Chamberlain, William ; 7 r Tournon
Chambers, George W.; 120 ave Wagram
Chandler, Mrs. W. S., Mondays ; 20 r Lesueur
Charette, General and Mde de ; 32 ave Hoche
Chase, Mr. and Mrs. A. H., Saturdays ; 3 r Washington
Cheritree, Miss Olive E.; 26 ave de la Grande-Armée
Cheronnet, Mr. and Mde ; 40 r Fortuny
Childe, Mr. and Mrs. Edward Lee ; 1 r François-Premier
Chotteau, Leon ; 138 bd Pereire
Christmas, Mrs. Richard ; 36 ave d'Iéna
Clarke, Mr. and Mrs. Charles Gordon ; 11 r Lincoln
Clements, G. H. ; Vannes
Cleveland, Mrs. Augustus ; 75 ave Champs-Elysées
Clinch, Mr. and Mrs. Charles J., Mondays ; address Drexell,
    Harjes & Co.
    Clinch, Stewart
    Clinch, Miss
Coëtlogon, Viscount and Viscountess Réné de ; 7 ave du Bois
    de Boulogne
Cole, Miss Adelaide ; Hotel Balzac
Connolly, Mr. and Mrs. T. ; 5 ave de l'Opéra
Coolidge, J. T.; 140 bd St. Germain
Copeland, Alfred B.; Hotel Brisson
Corbin, Austin ; 40 r Fortuny
    Corbin, Mrs.

Corbin, Mr. and Mrs. Richard W. ; 7 ave Kléber
Correja, Henry ; 25 ave Villiers
Corryn, Henry ; 23 r de Boulogne
Cox, Kenyon ; 63 r de Seine
Crafts, Mr. and Mrs. James M. ; 76 ave du Trocadéro
 Crafts, Miss
Cram, Mr. and Mrs. Charles Warren, Saturdays ; 4 r Logelbach
Crane, Mr. and Mrs. Edward A., Wednesdays ; 1 r Pierre-Charron
Crane, Dr. and Mrs. John W. ; Saturdays ; 4 r Logelbach
Crawford, Kenneth ; 6 r Mayet
Creveling, Colonel and Mrs. H. C. ; 29 bd des Capucines
Cunst, Mr. and Mrs. O. C.; Hotel Danube, r Richepance
Currier, Alger ; 203 bd d'Enfer
Curtis, R. W. ; 13 r d'Aumale
Cutting, Mrs. Hayward ; 3 ave du Bois de Boulogne
 Cutting, Henry
 Cutting, Miss
Cutting, Mrs. T. B.; Hotel Liverpool
 Cutting, T. B., Jr.
 Cutting, William Jr.
Daboll, Dr. and Mrs. G. C. ; 14 ave de l'Opéra
Dana, Mr. and Mrs. Charles E.; 8 ave Hoche
Dana, S. H. ; 26 ave Friedland
 Dana, Miss
Dana, Mr. and Mrs. W. P. W., Fridays ; 12 r Presbourg
 Dana, Miss
 Noble, Mr. and Mrs..
Dannat, Mrs.; 123 ave Wagram
Dannat, William T.; 71 ave Villiers
Darcus, Dr. and Mrs.; 7 r Poisson
Davis, Charles H.; Fleury (Seine-et-Oise)
Day, Francis ; 203 bd d'Enfer
Deacon, Mr. and Mrs. Edward Parker ; 75 ave Champs-Elysées
Delmas, Mr. and Mrs. D. M.; 50 ave Kléber
Delprat, Mr. and Mrs. James, Saturdays ; 68 ave Kléber
 Delprat, Mr.

Demangeat, Mr. and Mrs. ; Avignon
Denman, H. F. ; 20 r d'Assas
Didot, Mr. and Mrs. Louis Gelis, Mondays ; 2 r Portalès
Dillon, H. P. ; 84 bd Rochechouart
Dodge, Mr. and Mrs. Edmund A. ; 210 r Rivoli
Dodson, Miss Sarah N. B. ; 112 bd Malesherbes
Dolph, J. ; address Goupil & Co.
Donaldson, Mr. and Mrs. Alexander; address 10 bd Sébastopol
Donoghue, John ; 188 r Vanves
Donoho, Ruger ; 23 r Tournon
Dortic, Mr. and Mrs. Henry T., Wednesdays ; 8 r Lamennais
Dressner, Ernest T. E. ; 127 ave de Paris
Dreyfus, Mr. and Madame ; 3 ave Ruysdale
    Dreyfus, Auguste
Druilhet, Madame ; 61 ave Kléber
    Druilhet, J. A.
Du Bos, Mr. and Madame A. ; 3 r Christophe-Colomb
Dufais, Mr. and Mrs. Ferdinand F. ; Hotel de l'Amirauté
Dunbar, Mrs., Saturdays ; 1 r Cadiz
    Dunbar, Miss
Dupuy, Dr. and Mrs. Eugene ; 85 ave Montaigne
Dyer, Dr. and Mrs. Charles Gifford ; 44 r Villejuif
Eakin, Mrs. Thomas, Saturdays ; 37 r de la Pelouze
    Ewing, Mrs.
Edwards, J. W. ; 147 ave Villiers
Emont, Anna de ; 28 r Faubourg St. Honoré
Erlanger, Baron and Baroness ; 20 r Taitbout
Estrada, Mlle. Gutierrez de, Wednesdays ; 24 r François-Premier
Evans, Dr. and Mrs. John ; 19 ave de l'Opéra
Evans, Dr. and Mrs. Theodore S. ; 18 bd Maillot, Neuilly
Evans, Mr. and Mrs. Theodore W. ; 17 bd de la Madeleine
Evans, Mr. and Mrs. Thomas W., Sundays and Tuesdays ; 99 ave
    Malakoff
Fagnani, Mrs. Emma, Wednesdays ; 22 Place Vendôme
    Fagnani, Miss
    Everett, Miss

Fairchild, Miss ; 30 r Galilée
Fassit, Francis Louis ; 20 r Mazarine
Faulds, James Sheridan ; 108 ave Champs-Elysées
Fetridge, Pembroke W., Sundays ; 13 ave du Bois de Boulogne
    Fetridge, Henry Pembroke
    Fetridge, Miss
    Fetridge, Miss Florence
Fevez, Mrs., Thursdays ; 20 r Cambacérès
    Hickson, Mrs. ; 3 r du Cirque
Filloneau-Yapp, Mde ; 3 place Wagram
Finn, I. H. ; 203 Bd d'Enfer
Fisher, Mr. and Mrs Joseph ; 26 ave Friedland
    Fisher, Mrs. Robert
Fisher, Mr. and Mrs. Frank C., Saturdays ; 49 r Lisbonne
Fithian, Mr. and Mrs. Joel ; 54 r Monceau
Flagg, H. P. ; 53 *bis* quay Grands-Augustins
Flagg, Montague ; 74 r de Seine
Flattery, Mr. and Mrs. Walter J. ; 17 place de la Madeleine
Forbes, Mr. and Mrs. Paul S. ; 53 ave de l'Alma
    Forbes de Courcy
    Forbes, Charles S.
    Forbes, Miss
    Forbes, Miss Pauline
Foster, J. H. ; 10 r de la Trémoille
Fox, C. S. ; 13 r Tocqueville
France, Miss Jessie L. ; 220 bd d'Enfer
Franklin, Mrs. Admiral ; 30 rue Bassano
Freeman, Mr. and Mrs. William ; 69 ave de l'Opéra
Funck-Brentano, Charles ; 5 r la Barouillère
Furness, Miss Rebecca F. ; 30 r Vaugirard
Gabriac, Count and Countess de ; 23 r des Bassins
Gallatin, Mrs. Albert Louis ; 14 r Pierre-Charron
Gardner, Miss Elizabeth J. ; 73 r Notre-Dame-des-Champs
Gardnier, Henry ; 65 r Saintonge
Garesché, Miss Anna, Tuesdays ; 15 r Presbourg
    Garesché, Miss

Garesché, Miss Lise
Garrett, E. H. ; 140 ave Villiers
Gay, Walter ; 11 r Daubigny
Gibb, Mr. and Mrs. Howard, Mondays ; 32 ave de l'Opéra
Gibin, George ; 6 r Chartreuse .
Giles, Mr. and Mrs. Fayette S. ; 45 r Clichy
    Giles, Miss
Giles, Mrs. Henry, Friday ; 8 r de l'Université
    Giles, Spencer
    Giles, Murray
    Giles, Miss
    Giles, Miss Helen
Gilman, B. F. ; 2 r Thénard
Gillig, Henry F. ; 35 bd des Capucines
Godwin B. ; 30 r Faubourg St. Honoré
Glatz, Mde Veuve Léon, Thursdays ; 45 r Clichy
Goldner, Mr. and Mrs. W., Fridays ; 93 r de la Pompe, Passy
Gompertz, Mde Veuve ; 51 ave Marceau
Good, Dr. ; 23 ave Bois de Boulogne
Goodridge, Francis ; 2 r Lincoln
    Goodridge, Miss
Gorisson, Mr. and Mrs. Albert von ; 1 ave Montaigne
Götendorf, James Jr. ; 9 rue Bergère
Götendorf, S. N. ; 39 r Clichy
Götz, M. and Mde Léon, Tuesdays ; 53 r Lisbonne
    Götz, Miss
Grayson, C. P. ; 35 r de Seine
Gregory, Eliot ; in America
Griffin, Francis Fiske ; 35 r Notre-Dame-des-Champs
Griswold, Mr. and Mrs. A. Minor, Fridays ; 2 ave Friedland
Groff, Dr. and Mrs., Wednesdays ; 24 ave Carnot
    Groff, William N.
    Groff, Miss
Gross, P. A. ; 7 r Chaptal
Gueydam, Madame F. ; 67 ave Kléber
Gurnee, Mr. and Mrs. Walter E. ; 26 ave Champs-Elysées

Gutherz, Mr. and Mrs. Carl ; 17 ave Gourgeaud

Haggarty, Mrs. ; 76 ave Trocadéro

Hall, Mrs. Basil ; 211 r St. Honoré

Hall, Dr. and Mrs. Charles O.; 5 r de la Paix

Hall, Miss Ellen D.; 2 r Thénard

Hall, Henry C.; 13 r Auber

Hardie, R. S.; 71 ave Villiers

Harjes, Mr. and Mrs. John, Mondays ; 62 ave Henri-Martin
    Harjes, Miss

Harrison, Alexander ; 72 r Notre-Dame-des-Champs

Hart, Benjamin ; 60 r de la Victoire

Harting, General and Mde ; 9 bd Latone

Harwood, Bert; 203 bd d'Enfer

Hastings, Thomas ; 13 r l'Observatoire

Hawley, Mr. and Mrs. Charles E.; 59 r des Mathurins
    Hawley, Miss

Haviland, Maurice ; 1 r de la Vera

Haynie, Henry 5 r Robert-Estienne

Healy, Mr. and Mrs. G. P. A., Thursdays ; 66 r de la Roche-
    foucauld
    Healy, Miss
    Healy, Miss Kathleen
    Bigot, Mr. and Mrs.
    Lamar, Mr. and Mrs.

Heaton, A. J.; 155 r faubourg St. Honoré

Heath, Mrs. W. G.; 6 r de Presbourg
    Hunt, William
    Hunt, Wilson G.

Hecht, Hein ; 60 r de la Victoire

Hein, Mr. and Mrs. O. L.; Hotel du Pavillon de Rohan

Heine, Mr. and Madame Michel; 21 ave Hoche
    Heine, George
    Heine, Madame Charles

Hellman, Mr. and Mrs. Max, Tuesdays; 12 r Dumont-d'Urville
    Hellman, Miss
    Hellman, Miss Nellie

Hemert, Mr. and Mrs. Charles Auguste von ; 14 r Lincoln
Heerman-Hundertmarck de, Dr. Charles and Mrs. de, Wednesdays;
      62 r Pierre-Charron
      Heermann, Clifford
      Heermann, Charles
      Heermann, Valentine
      Heermann, Miss
Herrick, Mr. and Mrs. William K.; 7 r Lisbonne
      Herrick, Misses
Her, Dr. and Mrs. Cornelius; 37 ave Kléber
Hewitt, Mrs. O.; 203 bd d'Enfer
      Hewitt, Miss
Hime, Mr. and Mrs. Douglas; 44 ave Victor Hugo
Hinckley, Robert ; 54 r Notre-Dame-des-Champs
Hirschberger, Carl; 6 r des Chartreux
Hobson. J. H. ; 35 bd des Capucines
Hocmélle, Robert ; 3 r Mancini
Hodge, Mrs. ; 14, r Pierre-Charron
Hodge, Miss ; 21 r Lafitte
Hoeminghaus, Mr. and Mrs. Fritz ; 26 r Washington (cité Odiot)
Hoffman, Mr. and Mrs. Charles B. ; 24 r Bassano
      Hoffman, Miss
Homans, Mr. and Mrs. Henry S ; 19 ave de l'Opéra
      Warren, Miss
Holman, Francis ; 203 bd d'Enfer
Hooper, Mr. and Mrs. Robert M., Saturdays; 76 r des Petits-Champs
      Hooper, Robert M., jr.
      Hooper, Miss
Hooper, Mrs. William ; 3 r de Tilsit
      Hooper, Miss
      Twombley, Douglas
      Twombley, William
Hopkins, Miss Florence ; 10 r St. Philippe-du-Roule
Hopkins, Mrs. T. M. ; 30 r Faubourg St. Honoré
Horroch, Mr. and Mrs. de, Saturdays ; 4 r Général Foy
Hottinger, Baron and Baroness ; 82 bd Malesherbes

Hough, Rev. Dr. J. W.; Hotel Campbell, ave Friedland
Howe, William H.; 157 ave Wagram
Howland, Mrs. John; 22 ave Kléber
    Flandin Miss
Hunt, Mr. and Mrs. Richard Howland; 3 r de la Planche
Hunter, William C.; 8 r Bassano
Huntington, Mrs. H. A., Mondays; 5 r de Beaune
    Huntington, Major Henry A.
    Huntington, Douglas St. George
    Huntington, Miss
Huppert, Edmund A.; 203 bd d'Enfer
Hutchinson, Mr. and Mrs. Alexander, Fridays; 32 r de Tocqueville
    Hutchinson, Alexander
    Hutchinson, Miss
Hutchinson, Mr. and Mrs. Bernard; Montargis
Ives, Mr. and Mrs. Albert C., Fridays; 37, r de Lille
Jackson, Mrs. J.; 15 ave d'Antin
Jackson, Madame J. C.; 8 bis ave Bois de Boulogne
Jameson, Mr. and Mrs. Conrad; 115 bd Malesherbes
Jarosson, Mrs. L., Sundays; 5 r Bassano
    Jarrosson, Miss
Jauregay, Esteban; 20 r Mazarine
Jay, Mr. and Mrs. Augustus, Fridays; 70 ave Marceau
Jeançon, Miss Blanche; 59 r des Sablons, (Passy)
Jenkins, Mr. and Mrs. George C; 30 r Bassano
Jewett, Miss Mary; 12 bis r Descombes
Johnson, Mrs. W. E.; in London
Jones, F. C.; New York
Jones, Mrs. L. F.; 7 r Poisson
Jones, Colonel de Lancey Floyd; Hotel du Palais
Johnston, Mr. and Mrs. Charles Edward, Thursdays; 40 ave Marceau
Johnston, Mr. and Mrs. I., Thursdays; 14 r de Tilsit
    Johnston, Misses
Joslin, W. L.; 35 r Cambon
Kane, John C.; 11 bd Malesherbes

Kelly, Mr. and Mrs. Edmond ; 21 r Auber

Kern, Alexander ; 19 r Cambacérès

Kerr, Mr. and Mrs. William J. Saturdays ; 93 ave Henri-Martin

Kernochan, Mr. and Mrs. W. S. ; 25 r de Marignan

Kessler, Count and Countess, Mondays; 30 cours la Reine

Ketson, A. H. ; 17 r Notre-Dame-des-Champs

Kindelberger, D. ; 30 r du Faubourg St. Honoré

King, Edward ; 96 ave des Ternes
    Fisher, Misses

King, Emma C. ; 19 quai St. Michel

King, Mrs. George, Thursdays ; 10 ave Wagram
    Contour, Mrs.

King, Miss Henrietta L. ; 19 r Ecuries-d'Artois
    King, Miss

King, James S. ; 35 r de Seine

Klenck, Baroness de, Wednesdays; 26 ave Marceau

Klumpke, Mrs. D. M., First and Third Thursdays ; 88 bd St. Michel
    Klumpke, William
    Klumpke, Miss
    Klumpke, Augusta
    Klumpke, Mathilda
    Klumpke, Julia

Knight, D. R. ; place de l'Église, Poissy

Kohn, E. ; 21 bd Montmartre

La Beaume, Mde Hicks ; 39 r Général-Foy
    La Beaume, Miss

La Fonta, Mr. and Mrs. E. ; 30 r St. Petersburg

Lamb, F. S. ; 39 r d'Orsel

Lamontagne, Mr. and Mrs. August ; 70 ave Kleber
    Lamontagne, C.
    Lamontagne, Miss
    Lamontagne, Miss Elisabeth

Lamson, Mrs. John, Thursdays ; 39 r Galilée
    Draper, George H.

Lancey, Ward de ; 198 r de Courcelles

Larpenteur, James D.; St. Paul, Minnesota
Lash, L. W.; 7 r de Tournon
Lawrence, Miss Jennie O.; 4 r Balzac
Lazard, Mr. and Mrs. Simon ; 10 ave de Messine
Lecesne, Mr. and Mrs. Charles; 45 ave Marceau
    Lecesne, Miss
Lecesne, Mr. and Mrs. William; 38 r des Mathurins
Legay, Mr. and Mrs. Charles, 24 r Boccador
Leighton, George W.; 32 *bis* bd Haussmann
Ledoux, Mde Amaron, Thursdays; 12 r de Presbourg
Lee, Mrs. M. W.; 167 bd Pereire
Lemmon, Miss; 15 r des Bassins
Leroy, Mr. and Mrs. R.; 70 ave d'Iena
Lesieur, Mde., Tuesdays; 23 r Chaussée-d'Antin
Lesley, Miss W. M.; 2 r Thénard
Lherbette, Charles; 19 r Scribe
Lillie, Mr. and Mrs. Andrew D.; 16 r Pierre-Charron
Limet, Félix ; 36 *bis* ave de l'Opéra
Loomis, Chester; Paint Rock, Texas
Loubat, J. F. ; 47 r Dumont-d'Urville
Lowrey, Mr. and Mrs. John S.; Hotel Bristol
Lucas, Mr. and Mrs. George C. ; 34 ave Trocadéro
    Lucas, Albert
    Lucas, Miss
    Lucas, Miss Mary
    Lucas, Miss Laura
    Middleton, Mr. and Mrs. Stanley
Lucas, George L.; 21 r l'Arc-de-Triomphe
Lucas, S. R. ; 11 r Lord Byron
Luckhardt, Mr. and Mrs. J. H. ; 78 r Peronnet, Neuilly
Lyman, Mr. and Mrs. Charles ; 21 r Weber
Machado, Mr. and Mrs. J. N.; Mondays; 28 ave Marceau
Mackay, Mr. and Mrs. John W., Tuesdays ; 9 r de Tilsit
    Colonna di Galatro, Prince and Princess
MacMonness ; 11 imp du Maine
MacNeil, C. A. ; 89 bd Strasbourg

Macteer, Mr. and Mrs. Alexander ; 28 ave Montaigne
Main, Mrs. O. O. ; 8 r Presbourg
    Brydon, Mrs.
    Brydon, Miss
Main, Miss Julia ; 59 ave Kléber
Marborough-Lara, Comte and Comtess de ; 23 r des Bassins
Marcy, W. L.; 164 bd Montparnasse
Marcy, Miss ; 16 r Christophe-Colombe
Marston, William A. ; 32 ave Marceau
Martin, Miss ; 3 *bis* r Galilée
    Martin, Miss Fanny B.
Martin, Mr. and Mrs. Francisco de F. ; 2 r Euler
Mathews, Arthur F. ; 12 r de Seine
Mayer, Ernest ; address Am.-Ex. 35 bd des Capucines
McAfee, Mr. and Mrs. L. C. ; 85 ave Montaigne
McDougall, J. A., jun. ; 9 r de l'Orient
McDowell, E. W. ; 6 r des Chartreux
McEwen, Walter ; address Meadows & Co., r Scribe
McGruder, Mr. and Mrs. George A. ; 24 r Ecuries-d'Artois
McKaye, Colonel and Mrs. James, Saturdays ; 1 r Pierre-Charron
McLane, Hon. and Mrs. Robert M , Fridays ; 70 ave Marceau
McLean, Edward P. ; address 24 r du Quatre-Septembre
Melchers, Julius Gari ; 27 r Tournon
Meletta, Mr. and Mrs., Saturdays ; 71 ave Marceau
    Meletta, Charles A.
    Meletta, Louis
Mendell, Mr. and Mrs. Henry, Fridays ; bd Courcelles
Meslier, Mde. Amadée ; 4 passage de la Madeleine
    Meslier, Auguste
    Meslier, Victor
Meunier, Mr. and Mrs. Léon ; 53 r de Naples
Meynell, Mrs., Tuesdays ; 1 ave Bois de Boulogne
Miles, J. R. ; 66 r de Seine
Mills, Harry ; 29 r Laval
Miltenberger, Mr. and Mde. Alphonse, Thursdays ; 6 r Daubigny
Minturn, Mde. William, Fridays ; 90 ave Kléber

Mitchell, Guernsey; 23 r Faubourg St. Honoré
Moir, Mrs. E. J.; Thursdays; 204 r du Faubourg St. Honoré
    Moir, Miss
Monks, R.; address Munroe & Co.
Montmort, Marquise de; Hotel d'Albe
Moore, Mr. and Mrs. Charles M.; 170 ave Victor-Hugo
Moore, Mr. and Mrs. Humphrey, Saturdays, 4 *to* 6; 55 ave des
    Ternes, passage Doisy
Moore, Mr. and Mrs. W. J.; 32 ave Marceau
Monlun, Mr. and Mrs. Henry, Saturdays; 27 r Galilée
    Monlun, P.
    Monlun, H. E.
    Monlun, Miss
    Monlun, Miss T. M.
Moreau, Mr. and Mde. H.; 370 r St. Honoré
Moorhouse, Mr. and Mrs. H. P.; 7 r Paradis
    Moorhouse, Miss
    Moorhouse, Miss Lottie
Mosler, Mr. and Mrs. Henry, Saturdays; 12 r la Tremoille
Moss, C. E.; 34 r de la Fontaine-St.-Georges
Moss, Frank; 13 r Laval
Mounsey, Mrs. A. H.; 38 ave Montaigne
Mowbray, H. H.; 7 r de Tournon
Munsell, Mr. and Mr. A. H.; 32 r de Vaugirard
Nachtel, Dr. Henry; 5 r Castiglione
Nettleton, Walter; 33 r Jacob
Newmann, Carl; Hotel d'Angleterre, r Jacob
Nivin, Mrs. Robert J.; 58 r Galilee
Nugent, J. M. 3 r Bonaparte
O'Connor, Mr. and Mrs. James; 32 ave d'Iéna
O'Connor, Mrs. John, Tuesdays; 55 ave Marceau
    O'Connor, Miss
    O'Connor, Miss Agnes
O'Halloran, J. J.; 2 r Odessa
Oglesby, Mrs., Wednesdays; 4 r Balzac
Osgood, Miss W. K.; 36 r Saint-Ferdinand

Palengat, Mr. and Mrs. Pierre; 3 r Copernic
Palmer, Mde.; 59 r Galilée
 Palmer, Miss
Parker, Charles S.; 33 r de Tournon
Parker, Mrs. William, Thursdays; 17 r d'Athènes
Parker, Stephen H.; 64 r de La Rochefoucauld
Parmely, Mr. and Mrs. George W.; 2 r Pierre-Charron
Pearce, Charles Sprague; Auvers (Seine-et-Oise)
Pell, Mrs. Walden, Fridays; 1 ave Montaigne
Penfield, F. C.; Port-Aven (Finistère)
Pennie, R. M.; 14 r Navarin
Penniman, Mrs. Charles P.; 75 ave des Champs-Elysées
 Penniman, Charles
Pennington, R. G. H.; 15 r Boissonnade
Perkins, Charles Bruen; 66 r de Seine
Perkins, Mr. and Mrs. Edward N., Fridays; 9 bd de la Madeleine
Perkins, F.; 5 Villa Saint-Michel
Perreau, Mr. and Mrs.; 32 ave Marceau
Peters, Clinton; 4 r Luxembourg
Peters, C. R.; 7 r Tournon
Phalen, Mrs.; 23 r des Bassins
Post, Miss; 3 r Copernic
 Post, Miss Lena
Post, Wright E.; 23 r Marignan
Poucher, W. E.; address Munroe & Co.
Pratt, Dr. and Mrs. Thomas; 12 place Vendôme
 Pratt, Miss
Preston, Mde.; 11 r Portalis
 Preston, Miss
Radcliff, Mr.; 109 bd Haussmann
 Radcliff, Miss
Randolph, Mrs.; 2 r Lincoln
Rantoul, Robert S.; 7 r du Colisée
Raught, John; 66 r de Seine
Reinhart, Mr. and Mrs. C. S., Fridays; 75 ave Villiers
 Reinhart, A. G.

Reitlinger, Adolph H.; 65 r d'Anjou
Reubell, Mr. and Mrs.; 42 r Gabriel
    Reubell, Miss
Reutlinger, Emile ; 21 bd Montmartre
Reyman, Adolph ; 103 ave Neuilly
Ribon, Mr. and Mrs. J. G. ; 36 ave d'Iéna
    Ribon, Thomas Germon
    Ribon, Rafael
    Ribon, Miss
Rich, Mr. and Mrs. J. P., Fridays; 10 r Poisson
Rich, Thomas P.; 55 r de la Grande-Chaumière
Richards, Mrs. , 28 r Bassano
    Richards, William S.
    Richards, Miss
    Richards, Miss Elise
Richardson, Frank H. ; 10 r Croix des Petits-Champs
Rhees, M. G. ; 7 r Tou.non
Rhodes, Albert ; 35 r Cambon
Ribot, Mr. and Mrs. Alexander; 65 r Jouffroy
Ridgway, Mde.; 5 r François-Premier
Riggs, Mrs. Joseph K.; 66 ave d'Iéna
Riggs, Mr. and Mrs. William H.; 13 r Murillo
Ritchie, Colonel and Mrs. Harrison; 5 r Tilsit
    Ritchie, Miss
Robb, Mr. and Mrs. G. H.; in America
    Walsh, Miss
Robbins, Mrs., Wednesdays 4 p m. Sundays 5 p.m.; 4 r Presbourg
    Robbins, Miss
Robbins, Miss Lee; 17 quai d'Orsay
Robertson, R. Austin; 50 r Courcelles
Robin, Mr. and Mrs. Theodore ; 16 r Vigny
Rochereau, Mr. and Mrs. Eugene, Tuesdays; 140 bd Haussmann
    Rochereau, Miss
Roe, Mr. and Mrs. Frederick A.; 18 r Belloy
    Roe, Miss
Rogers, Mrs. E. D.; 20 ave Carnot

Rogers, Miss
Rogers, Dr. H.; 1 r du Havre
Ryan, Dr.; 25 r Royale
Ryder, Henry O. ; 57 r de Lille
Ruckstuhl ; 203 bd d'Enfer
Roques, Mrs. von ; 12, r Bassano
Rudy, Charles ; 7 r Royale
Russell, Mrs. William H. ; 48 ave Gabriel
Ryan, Mrs. J. J., Wednesdays ; 13 r
Salmon, Mr. and Mde. Adolph ; 70 r Hauteville
Salvador, Baron and Baroness, Saturdays ; 11 r Traktir
Sanderson, Miss Mabel ; 30 r Bassano
      Sanderson, Miss
Sandford, Mr. and Mrs. Louis H. ; 11 *bis* r Portalis
Santry, Daniel François ; 15 r Jacob
Sargent, John S. ; in London
Sass, George ; 66 r Notre-Dame-des-Champs
Sauville, Madame de ; 41 bd Berthier
Schemerhorn, Mrs. E. ; 32 ave Trocadéro
Schlesinger, Louis ; 58 r Pierre-Charron
Schreiner, Mrs. Horace A. ; 39 r Galilée
      Schreiner, Miss
Scott, Charles N. ; 22, r de l'Arcade
Seker, C. H. ; 21 ave Carnot
Seligman, Mr. and Mrs. William, Wednesdays ; 26 ave Villiers
      Seligman, Antoine
      Seligman, Percy
      Seligman, Miss
Seligman, Mr. and Mrs. David, Saturdays ; 12 r Vigny
Shean, Charles M. ; 49 r Denfert-Rochereau
Shephard, Mrs. E. C. ; 3 r Ponthieu
      Shephard, Miss
Shepherd, J. H. D.; 8 r Mondovi
Shillito, Mr. and Mrs. Gordon ; 23 ave Bois de Boulogne
Shonborn, J. L. ; Montleveque (*près* Senlis)
Simmons, Mr. and Mrs. Edward E. ; 140 ave Villiers

Simons, Marius ; 18 r du Bois de Boulogne
Slader, Mr. and Mrs. ; 23 ave Henri-Martin
Smedley, V. N. ; 3 r Bonaparte
Smith, de Cost ; 38 r Ramey
Smith, E. B. ; 5 r Douai
Smith, Miss Helen W. S. ; 146 ave Champs-Elysées
Smith, John Lewis ; r de la Fontaine-St.-George
Smith, Miss Sarah Ida ; 36 r St. Ferdinand
Snelling, Mr. and Mrs. Edward Templeton, Fridays ; 4 r Balzac
    Snelling, Grenville Temple
Soneel, Louis ; 3 r du Bac
Snow, Miss Clara ; 3 r du Bac
Somerville, Mr. and Mrs. Lionville, Saturdays ; 1 r Pierre-Charron
Southgate, Mr. and Mrs. Frederick ; 118 r Lafayette
Sorchan, Mr. and Mrs. M. A., Fridays ; 10 r Lincoln
    Sorchan, Victor
    Sorchan, Miss
Spaulding, Mr. and Mrs. H. A., Fridays ; 39 r du Général-Foy
    Spaulding, Russell
    Spaulding, Miss
Spencer, Mr. and Mrs. Henry W., Fridays ; 32 r de Verneuil
Spencer, Charles ; 70 *bis* r Notre-Dame-des-Champs
Spencer, Mr. and Mrs. Lorillard ; 36 ave d'Iéna
    Spencer, Lorillard jr.
Sperry, Mrs. S. C. ; 54 r Galilée
Springer, Miss Eda ; 59 ave Kléber
Stark, Otto ; 6 r Chapelais
Stern, Mrs. Edward ; 61 ave Kléber
Sterner, Albert E. ; 29 r Laval
Stewart, Edward ; 15 r Jacob
Stewart, Julius L.; 36 r Copernic
Stewart, Mr. and Mrs. William H., Tuesdays ; 6 ave d'Iéna
    Stewart, William H., jr.
    Stewart, Miss
Stickney, Mr. and Mrs. J. D. ; address 1 r du Havre
Stout, Miss ; 27 r Victor-Hugo

St. Amant, Mr. and Mrs. George, Wednesdays; 154 bd Haussmann
Strickland, Mr. and Mrs. John W. A., Saturdays; 36 ave d'Iéna
    Strickland, C. Hobart
    Strickland, Miss
    Strickland, Miss Mattie
    Allen, Miss
Strong, Mrs. Charles; 61 ave d'Antin
Sturgis, Mr. and Mrs., Wednesdays; 146 ave des Champs-Elysées
    MacLeod, Miss
Sutliffe, Albert; address 24 r Quatre-Septembre
Taber, Mr. and Mrs. James A.; 1 r Pierre-Charron
    Taber, Miss
Thaxter, Miss Percy; 2 r Thénard
Thebaud, Mrs. Jules; 70 ave d'Iéna
    Thebaud, Miss
    Thebaud, Miss Josephine
    Thebaud, Miss Marie
    Thebaud Miss Eugenia
    Webb, Mr. and Mrs.
Theriat, Mrs. C. J.; 83 ave Marceau
    Theriat, Miss
Thirion, Charles F.; 24 r du Quatre-Septembre
Thompson, Mr. and Mrs.; 8 r Presbourg
Thorburn, Miss, Fridays; 69 ave Marceau
Thorndike, Stewart; 48 ave Gabriel
    Thorndike, Miss
Thwing, Mr.; 41 ave Kléber
    Thwing, Misses
Tompkins, Miss Clementina; 11 bd Clichy
Trobriand, Countess de; 47 ave Champs-Elysées
Truesdell, C. S.; 3 r Campagne-Première
Tudor, Mrs. William; 14 r Châteaubriand
Tuckerman, Mr. and Mrs. Charles K.; 18 ave Kléber
    Tuckerman, Mr. and Mrs.
Tuke, H. S.; 2 r Odessa
Turner, Mr. and Mrs. Robert A., Fridays; 23 r Galilée

Turner, Edgar Ernest
Vail, Mr. and Mrs. L. E., Tuesdays ; 34 ave Trocadéro
 Vail, Eugene L.
 Vail, George
Valois, Mr. and Mrs. Arthur E.; 20 r Daunou
Van Bergen, Mr. and Mrs. A. ; 118 ave Champs-Elysées
Vanderpoel, John H.; 3 r Bonaparte
Van Trump, Misses; 11 r Boissonade
Vaughan, Mrs. George ; 165 r de l'Université
 Vaughan, Miss
Verrier, Miss ; 9 r Balzac
 Verrier, Miss Helena
Very, Mr. and Mrs. Edward V.; address 21 r Royale
Vielé, Mrs. ; 26 ave Marceau
 Vielé, Miss
Vignaud, Mr. and Mrs. Henry; 59 r Galilée
Vogel, Miss ; ave Carnot
 Vogel, Miss Alice
 Vogel, Miss Anna
 Vogel, Miss Christina
Wagner, Mrs. ; 5 bd de Courcelles
 Barnard, E.
Walden, Lionel ; 18 impasse du Maine
Walkeley, B. D. ; 87 r Rochechouart
Walker, Mr. and Mrs. George, Mondays ; 8 r Clément-Marot
 Walker, Miss
 Walker, Miss Anna
Ward, Mrs. Montague, Wednesdays ; 198 r Courcelles
Warren, Dr. Edward Bey, Wednesdays; 15 r Caumartin
 Warren, Miss
 Warren, Miss Inness
Warren, Mr. and Mrs. Whitney ; 1 r Lincoln
 Warren, Miss
Wasserman, Dr. and Mrs. Max, Fridays ; 17 r Phalsbourg
Watts, Russell, Very Rev. Michael, C.D. ; 50 ave Hoche
Weeks, E. L. ; 128 ave Wagram

Wewarden, John ; 20 r Mazarine
Wheeler, Mr. and Mrs. Davenport ; 22 r Lincoln
Whidden, William ; 83 r du Bac
Whiteing, Mrs. Richard ; 182 r Faubourg St. Honoré
Whiteman, J. Edwin ; 8 r Hyacinthe St. Honoré
Whitney, Dr. and Mrs. Thomas H., jr., Fridays ; 45 r St. Didier
Wickenden, R. J. ; 9 r l'Université
Wight, Mr. and Mrs. M. ; 49 bd Rochechouart
Wilbour, Mr. and Mrs. C. B., Sundays ; 164 bd Haussmann
    Wilbour, Victor
    Wilbour, Miss
Wilkie, Dr. and Mrs. C. M. ; 7 ave Gourgeaud
    Wilkie, Miss
Wilkinson, Mrs. S. H., Wednesdays ; 50 r François-Premier
    Wilkinson, Miss
Williams, F. D. ; 35 *bis* r Fleurus
Williams, Miss L. L.; 54 r Laugier
Wilson, Edmund Russell ; 88 r du Bac
Wingard, Mr. and Mrs. Karl J., Wednesdays ; 82 ave Kléber
Winslow, Mrs. George S. ; Hotel Liverpool
    Winslow, Miss
Winthrop, Mrs. B. R. ; 12 Rond Point, Champs-Elysées
    Winthrop, Robert
Wolff, Otto ; 5 r de Laval
Woodward, Dr. H. C.; 26 r Washington
    Woodward, Miss
Woodward, Dr. J. J. ; 12 r Sommerard
Wood, Ogden ; 9 r Bochard-de-Sarron
Wright, F. E.; 16 r Boissonade
Wright, Mde. V. ; 14 r Pierre-Charron
    Wright, Mde. Hamilton
Wright, Mrs. Parkinson, Fridays ; 69 ave Marceau
    Thorburn, Miss
Wüertz, Emil ; 1 r de l'Ambre
Yeatman, Professor and Mrs. Thomas ; bd Victor Hugo, Parc de
    Neuilly

Yelland, Mr. and Mrs. ; 81 bd St. Michel
Yelland, Miss

LIST OF CHANGES AND CORRECTIONS.

Bogue, Dr. and Mrs. E. H. ; 39 bd Haussmann
Bullet, Miss ; 31 r Tocqueville
Hatheway, Dr. and Mrs. C. ; 17 ave l'Opéra
Henry, Mr. and Mrs. Edward ; 10 r Poisson
Newell, Rev. and Mrs. W. W. ; 80 r Prony
Salter, Mr.; Hotel de Tours, r Jacob
Schoyer, Mr. and Mrs. Frank; 95 r Monceau
Tarn, Mrs.; 23 bd Bois de Boulogne
Upde-Graff, T. T.; 12 ave l'Alma

NOTE.—Errors in the foregoing list can be corrected with a fine pen or hard and carefully sharpened pencil in the blank space following the name. Other corrections can if desired be made in the same manner on the blank pages which follow. The book can thus be made to serve the purpose of a private calling and address list, changes of residence or of calling days being entered in the proper place whenever they occur. The blank pages will also be found extremely useful for shopping notes or social memoranda in general. It has been thought best to include in the list the names of a few persons temporarily absent from Paris, of some that have recently returned to America, and of a very limited number intimately associated with the Colony socially or in religious or benevolent work.

AMERICAN ARTISTS AND ART STUDENTS.

American art followed the laws of lineage and national allegiance till the Revolution and for some time afterwards, that is it looked to England and not to France for its inspiration. Benjamin West came to London and may possibly have sketched in the Louvre. Stuart, Trumbull and Copley studied in England and lived there for many years. Allston came to Paris and, it is said, learned the figure with David. John Vanderlyn of South Carolina was the first American to visit Paris as an art-student in the general sense of the term, and the first to exhibit at the Salon then held in the Musée Napoléon. He therefore occupies the first place in the history of American art so far as it relates to France. His picture *Caius Marius among the Ruins of Carthage* was exhibited in 1808 just after the victories of Iena, Æuerstadt, Eylau and Friedland had culminated in the treaty of Tilsit, and Napoleon was at the height of his power. Tradition says that the Emperor himself remarked it when passing through the gallery with his suite and suggested that it be awarded a medal. His motives aside from intrinsic merit of the canvas are a matter of conjecture. It is certain that he wished to retain the friendship of the United States in order to prevent its intimacy with England and a personal compliment like this would tend to that result. It is possible that the fallen greatness which the painting suggested might have inspired a vision not unlike that of his death in exile at St. Helena. The picture still exists in New York but it has been the privilege of only one living artist, so far as known, the eminent Dean of the Guild in Paris to have seen it. Were it to be placed on exhibition contemporary opinion would doubtless be greatly divided regarding its merits. Vanderlyn returned to America soon afterwards and a long interval followed during which American artists occasionally flitted through Paris, looked at its art treasures and hurried on to Rome to which they had now transferred their affections. It was not till after 1830 that they began to come to Paris in small numbers for the purpose of study. They studied but did not exhibit at the Salon. Tradition does not say that they made the effort. Among them is mentioned a South Carolina artist named de Voe who died at Rome. Wyeth, the son of a Philadelphia clergyman a young man who is described by those who knew him as not gifted, studied portraiture, but finding himself at the end of his resources went to England to recoup his shattered fortunes. He tried the country towns with success. His methods of seeking patronage were peculiar. When he found himself fairly installed at a tavern he began looking admiringly at the head and face of the landlord in which, as he explained, he saw with the eye of an artist a singular combination of classic form and physical beauty. This he said he should esteem it a privilege to paint. The flattery blended in suitable proportions with business tact succeeded. Having painted the portraits of the landlord and his family he extended his efforts to the town officials in whom he discovered similar traits and whom he captured with equal ease. As a result of his tour he returned to Paris to pursue his studies a few months later richer by several hundred pounds. Healy came in 1834. Fraser a Kentucky artist arrived in 1835. Those who are familiar with some editions of Thackeray's works containing eccentric illustrations from his own pencil will probably recall the fact that he studied art in Paris about the period in question, and failing, happily for the world, chose the career of authorship. He associated as a student with the Americans then pursuing the same object and was exceedingly kind to Rossiter who was ill and in poverty even going so far as to act in the capacity of nurse to him for several days and nights. It is a pleasing reminiscence of a man who is generally credited by the world with being of a cold, satirical, unsympathetic character. Among the American artists who pursued their studies in Rome about this time or a little later were Buchanan Read and Chapman. Munich began to come into fashion at nearly the same time and for many years divided the honor with Paris or attracted an even larger number of students.

The Dean of the Artists. No one of the artists has been so long a member of the American Colony of Paris as the well-known portrait-painter, G. P. A. Healy, or for a period extending over a greater part of fifty years has been so conspicuous at the Salon. He came in 1834 and exhibited his first pictures in 1836, being the second American to win that distinction. Since that date he has exhibited constantly with the exception of some time passed at Rome and a few years spent in America. One of his first portraits was that of General Cass, United States Minister at the Court of Louis-Philippe. It was through him that he made the King's acquaintance. A grand ball was to be given at the Ministerial residence on the twenty-second of February, and a portrait of Washington was wanted to be placed between that of the King and Guizot as the principal decoration of the Salon. This Mr. Healy painted from an engraving of the Stewart portrait furnished by General Cass. The following morning the artist was sent for by the King who expressed great pleasure at having been in such good company the previous evening. He said that he wanted a portrait of Washington for his gallery at Versailles, and would like it from the pencil of the artist who he wished to have go to England and copy the Stewart portrait which had been painted for Mrs. Bingham of Philadelphia and presented to the Earl of Lansdowne. The King wrote to Geoffroy St. Hilaire French Minister at the Court of St. James to discover its whereabouts, but as he informed the artist in a subsequent interview, it was inaccessible, the Marquis of Lansdowne having quarrelled with his heirs, and sold all his personal property. The portrait had gone with the rest and according to reports deemed reliable

8

was at St. Petersburg. This was afterwards found to be an error. It had simply been stored in a London warehouse where by permission of the person in charge it was seen and copied. Its history was a strange one. It was bought at the sale in question by one who hoped to speculate on its personal and historic value. It was offered to Parliament which declined to purchase the likeness of the arch-American rebel, and was at one time in danger of being disposed of by that plebeian method of realizing money on unsalable articles, the raffle. It is now in possession of the heirs of the late John D. Lewis of London. Mr. Healy was afterwards commissioned by Louis-Philippe to paint the portraits of distinguished American statesmen. He went to America on this mission, and had the singular fortune to be present at the death bed of General Jackson. He painted the portraits of Jackson, Clay, Webster, Calhoun and other celebrated Americans that are now at Versailles and of Lord Ashburton who negotiated with Webster the famous treaty known by the names of the two principals. The last two were purchased by the United States Government and are now at Washington. Besides these, Mr. Healy has painted numerous Americans of distinction, several European sovereigns, diplomatists of all nations, and innumerable Frenchmen eminent in politics, science and literature. It has become something of a distinction to be illustrated by his pencil. A long list of social virtues forms a graceful appendage to an artistic reputation honorably won. He has a kind and sympathetic nature ever ready to respond to the appeals of compatriots in distress. He is a stranger to personal malice. He speaks only good, not of the dead alone, but of the living. He is furthermore a genial *raconteur* sifting through a retentive and highly responsive memory the golden reminiscences of a long and eventful lifetime.

An Opinion of American Art. The question of the future of American art is answered in a somewhat categorical manner as follows by Mario Proth a Paris critic who published a volume on the art department of the

Universal Exposition of 1878: "When the New World shall be no longer new, when the American people shall have cleared all its land, constructed almost all its railroads, built almost all its cities, when it shall have almost finished its fight for existence, when it shall refuse to receive European emigrants, when it shall be almost a people, when it shall have a history, traditions, leisure, when it shall invent less and dream more, it will have a school of art. Such, without circumlocution, is the impression which the American Salon leaves upon us, so small, of this so great power. We had already remarked in its industrial exposition something singularly characteristic, a recent invention imitating at will metal, wood or leather, and furnishing according to circumstances or according to the desire of the person desiring the article a bronze bust, an oaken peg, an authentic piece of Cordova tapestry, and I know not what else. So in the American department we see many similitudes of painting, forms of half-articulate speech, imitations of art more or less plausible. There are some works of talent, of talent a little maladroit, whose promise surpasses the performance; and a single *chef-d'œuvre*." The picture to which the writer thus alludes is one called "Solitude," a view of the open sea by W. P. W. Dana without moving object, only sea and sky. The other artists mentioned in the book in a complimentary manner are Miss Tompkins, Miss Dodson, Wylie, Hovenden, Ward, Gedney Bunce, Copeland, Colman, Tiffany, Brown, Homer, Gifford, Eaton, Howland, Miller, Healy, Sargent, Porter and Huntington. The writer completes the portion of his work devoted to American artists by promising in the dim future some sort of artistic distinction to the United States. America, he says, has a curiosity regarding art which it seeks to satisfy by purchasing not always in the most judicious manner. Its past, having been excessively practical, it has not as yet the intuitions of art and cannot therefore be possessed of the taste. American painters will achieve success on the sole condition that they preserve the irreverence for official teaching that had enabled them up to the period treated of to accomplish the combined result which the exposition revealed. This was written nearly ten years ago and the conditions have since entirely changed. The number of artists exhibiting at the Salon has more than doubled. New and strong men have come in and were the aggregate of work done by American artists to be estimated now either at the Salon or at a Universal Exposition where the terms of admission are more liberal the verdict would be more comprehensive as well as more generous.

Future of American Art. It is to be hoped that the time will never come when the Americans will invent less. It will do them no harm, perhaps, to dream more certainly not if it gives them what is called in modern phraseology a school of art. To have a school of art implies something more than the ability to paint; it means to paint with a sort of individuality made up of national peculiarities and characteristics; something novel which has been developed in a new manner with the growth of another civilization; a feeling of freshness and originality that comes from less known seas and skies, and an alien climate; in fact something that has not been entirely imitated but is in some manner newly suggested or invented. If the Americans are an ingenious people should not the inventive quality which they possess so largely assist in developing a school of art? They are not lacking in originality. A climate highly charged with electricity has given them a mobile temperament. They have imagination as shown in their literature and in the spirit of humor that pervades the nation. They are not deficient in intellectual force. What then is necessary to make them as great in art as in physical development and material resources? In the first place, time. Art is long and time is fleeting. It passes quickly but its results are slow. After the hurry and labor of settling and developing a new country there must come a period of relative repose when the intellect and imagination shall have their perfect opportunity. It is to be hoped that this will not be the intellectual stagnation that weighs so heavily on the masses of Europe. It is indeed certain it will not. There will then be leisure for artistic work. But something will still be wanting. That is what is sometimes called the artistic atmosphere in which certain countries of Europe are bathed, in which they are supposed to exist. In France and Italy the people have art about them from their infancy. They live and breathe it. They are born in the shadow of wonderful monuments. Their baby eyes open on statues of marvellous grace and pictures of strange beauty. They drink from splendid fountains and worship in churches that are triumphs of art in architecture. Fed upon art in default of food more nourishing to the body it becomes an instinct to those who think and imagine, while as for dreaming, there is ample time for it in lands whose avenues of labor are overcrowded. Men are not born under the same conditions in America. There life is bare of art though rich in comfort. They have not the same exquisite things about them from their birth. Their imagination has less to feed upon. But they have the imitative faculty finely developed. They have an extraordinary facility for putting artistic ideas into form. This has been conclusively shown by the improvements they have made in wood engraving, the American magazines being without a peer among the illustrated publications of the world. Here is the border-land of art and mechanics, and the success in it has not been merely that of imitation but of invention as well. Here is the talent for the part of art called technique. As for the imaginative phase of it, it may be said in a general way that a people that can produce poets and writers of romance can produce painters and sculptors. How great these can become is a question for time to answer. The Americans are accused of being too practical, the reproach implying that they are lacking in imagination. The practical mind indicates a sound mind in a sound body. It is unfortunate that it is so, if it is to prevent their success in art. Is it inevitable that the painter, as is sometimes said of the poet, should be a man of unbalanced intellect, in other words, a little insane? However this may be it seems hardly necessary to discuss the question farther, this brief statement comprising all that has thus far been said regarding the future of American artists. They are accredited with pluck, boundless energy, and a good degree of technical skill. They are told that the artistic instinct is yet to be developed in them. If their country has not now an artistic atmosphere it cannot be helped. Time may remedy the evil. But there is no reason why they should not have the artistic temperament combined with an amount of practical genius that will help to give it successful expression. The best results are to be hoped from their energy, their perseverance, their capacity for labor, their intelligence, if they preserve, in spite of the influences about them while abroad, the marked individuality which is the honorable and distinguishing trait of the American character.

Art Students and Art Life. American art-students come abroad with various objects, and sometimes with peculiar ideas of what they desire and how to accomplish it. They hope to finish their studies and return at the end of the year. Little can be done in that time even if they have had experience before leaving America. Some wish to pursue art as a profession, some are sent by the New York illustrated papers to study drawing, while many desire to qualify themselves as teachers in seminaries or in the higher departments of the public schools. There is always a considerable percentage poorly provided with means who find themselves at the end of the year, their objects unaccomplished, and in great pecuniary trouble. The mistake they have made is in not understanding what they had to do and having come at all, or in coming insufficiently provided. Others are embarrassed because they have not been able to resist the temptations of Paris. As soon as the student has established himself in comfortable quarters he enters the private studio of some distinguished artist from whom he receives occasional suggestions, or one of the public studios in which some eminent artists are professors. The amount of instruction in either case is limited. The professors come two or three times a week and pass the work of the students in hasty review making a few criticisms. The principal advantage which the students derive from this mode of life is drawing from living models and the ideas they gain from one another. In a few cases instruction is more specific. Male and female students are usually in separate ateliers. A certain price is paid per month, per quarter, or per year, the model and the privileges of the studio being included, the student furnishing his own material. There are two or three classes per day, morning, afternoon, and evening, the price including the whole or a part as desired. At the best studios it is one hundred francs per month for the entire day, or sixty for half a day, a considerable reduction being made for a longer term. At others where less advantages are offered the price is much lower. Women are charged more than men. A department of sculpture is connected with the larger schools. A preliminary examination in anatomy limits somewhat the attendance of foreign pupils at the National School of Fine Arts, at which nevertheless there are found numerous Americans. The number of American art-students in Paris already exceeds three hundred and is constantly increasing. They are more or less inconstant as concerns particular schools often passing from one to another several times during the season. They spend more or less time in copying at the Louvre or Luxembourg galleries in the interval of their studio work. In June they all disappear from Paris going to Belgium and Holland, or to the favorite resorts of artists in France. It is the custom of all artists who have studied in France to couple the name of their master with their own on public occasions. The list of French artists who have given lessons in the past to American pupils or are still doing so include David, Gros, Couture, Cabanel, E. Frère, Yvon, Bonnat, Carolus-Duran, Bouguereau, Français, Gérôme, Tony Robert-Fleury, Lefebvre, Picot, Ary Schaefer, Munkaczy, Boulanger, Yon, Laurens, Bastien-Lepage, Thoren, Pelouse, Gleyre, Meissonnier, Van Marcke, Barrias, Jacquesson de la Chevreuse, Dagnan, Humbert, Gervex, Guillemet, Giacometti, Courtois, Collin, Zamacois, R. de Madrazo, Colin, Dupré, and Morot. Henry Mosler has a studio in the rue du Faubourg St. Honoré at which there are found numerous American students. Miss Klumpke gives lessons at her private studio in the rue de la Grande-Chaumière. The atelier under the direction of Carl Rosa has recently been enlarged and is the only one that illustrates its lessons in anatomy by the practical dissection of dead bodies. The professors at this school include some of the most celebrated artists in Paris. The atelier of Carolus-Duran is on the boulevard Port Royal. That under the direction of Rollins is in the rue Notre-Dame-des-Champs. Another under the same management is in the impasse Hélène. E. E. Simmons an American artist receives pupils. Bonnat has a few at his private studio, and Morot, Henner, Benjamin Constant, Gerôme, Cormon, and other artists of distinction have under their instruction at their own or at the public ateliers more or less American pupils. Few of these artists receive any direct recompense, the reward, especially of those who receive American students, being in the patronage that comes to them indirectly through an extended acquaintance with wealthy travellers.

Cost of Living. The cost of living in Paris is of great importance to those who wish to come here to study art. It is what they please to make it, as in American cities. If one lives luxuriously he has to pay for it accordingly. One can fare comfortably at reasonable prices, and by economy, and leading a strictly bohemian existence, expenses can be brought down to an extremely low figure without suffering serious deprivation. With a young man the question is of less moment. He takes not unkindly to bohemian ways and if he is really in love with his art he bears hardships without murmuring. He leases, alone or with a friend, a room at a considerable altitude which is at the same time his studio and his home. Here he lives and regulates his expenses according to the length of his purse, expending very little except for rent which need not greatly exceed one-hundred dollars a year. For from one hundred and fifty to two hundred dollars artists may be very advantageously placed as regards altitude as well as quarter of the city, most of them preferring elevated localities like the vicinity of

Montparnasse and Montmartre. Comfortable rooms in furnished houses can be rented at from eight to fifteen dollars a month, the occupants living as they please. If a young artist is willing to live like the clerks or other petty employés in various branches of business in Paris who earn from fifteen to thirty dollars a month he can rent a room next the roof in almost any of the apartment houses in the residence quarters for from thirty to forty dollars a year and furnish it comfortably for fifty more. In this manner he saves the value of his furniture the first year, and afterwards pays a rent that is little more than nominal. It is supposed in this case that he is a student not needing a studio. Young lady students are more restricted in their choice, but can still live in Paris without the expenditure of a great deal of money. The figures already given will serve as a basis of calculation. If they have some knowledge of art they can rent studios like those described and live in them like the male students, or they can rent rooms in hotels or in apartment houses under similar conditions. In hotels their rooms are cared for. In apartment houses an arrangement can be made with the concierge or with some woman of the neighborhood to keep them in order, and if desired to perform the whole or a part of the duties of the *cuisine* for a trivial stipend. Two or more young ladies may combine for housekeeping on a small scale and live cheaply if not always as they would wish. Such a life does not include all the comforts to which Americans are accustomed at home, but it is brief as far as the student is concerned and is rendered more tolerable by the fact that he is quite as well off as nine-tenths of the French whom he sees about him. The standard of comfort in France is quite different from that in the United States, and it will not harm the American art-student to learn something of this difference by practical experiment. Board in *pensions* varies from seven to ten dollars or more a week according to room or other advantages. To this amount must be added fuel, lights and other incidental expenses. This manner of living costs more, but if the student is not too much distracted by the society into which he is thrown, it enables him to devote himself entirely to his studies. Society,

especially American society, is always a dangerous distraction to
American students who desire to pursue art seriously in Paris.
They have opportunities which they are far from appreciating
while abroad, to wit, the learning of foreign languages, the
knowledge they may gain of foreign customs, and, what is most
desirable, a thorough comprehension of foreign systems and ideas
of art. These requisites can best be obtained in France by
association with French artists, and satisfactory association of
that character is only possible to those who have a command of
the French language. American students ought to study and
speak French on every possible occasion, and it is a question
whether to do this they should not to a great extent forego the
society of their compatriots and avoid the places where English is
chiefly spoken. This would lessen rather than increase the
dissipation among them and be found exceedingly profitable in its
final results. The information and suggestions regarding modes of
life in this paragraph apply only to those to whom economy is
not only a virtue but a necessity. There are many rich Americans
who come to Paris and pursue art not with the most admirable
results. There are others equally favored by fortune who study
art from the love of it and if the success they achieve is not
always commensurate with the effort they have made the art
education they have acquired is an ample compensation.

List of Artists and Students. The list that follows includes the
names of artists and art-students. No
other arrangemet was possible, persons
often continuing their studies years after they have exhibited at
the Salon or practiced their art in America. It was the intention
to include all who have studied in Paris during the past year but
many could not be found after the most careful effort. The
omissions number nearly a hundred. The places whence they
come are not given. It is only necessary to say that were they
added every state and city would be represented. Most come
from New York. That is an accident of population. Then come,

in the order in which the names stand, Philadelphia, Boston, St. Louis, Cincinnati and Chicago. San Francisco is always represented by a large delegation. Texas and Oregon furnish their quota, while not a few are from country villages in the Western States so remote from the great centers of civilization that it seems strange an esthetic idea should have rippled their stagnant life and sent one of their number across the Atlantic to study art in Europe.

LIST OF ARTISTS AND ART STUDENTS.

Adams, S. Herbert ; 39 r l'Ambre
Albright, Adeline ; 10 r St. Hyacinthe
Allen, W. S. ; 7 ave du Trocadéro
Allen, Thomas ; Ecouen (Seine-et-Oise)
Anderson, A. A., 5, Passage Saulnier
Anderson, David J.; 7 r Tournon
Andrews, Mrs. ; 9 ave McMahon
Arter, J. C. ; 35 r Cambon
Babcock, W. P. ; Barbizon
Bacon, Henry, Saturdays ; 157 r Faubourg St. Honoré
Baird, W. B. ; 3 r Odessa
Baker, Ellen K. ; 11 r Lemaître-Puteaux
Baldwin, Esther ; Hotel Balzac
Barber, Alice ; 50 r Faubourg St. Denis
Barlow, J. N. ; 17 r du Départ
Barnesley, J. M. ; 4 r Aumont-Thiéville
Barse, George E. jr. ; 7 r Alfred Stevens
Bartlett, T. W. ; 104 r Blomet
Beals, W. H., 7 r Tournon
Beckwith, J. C., 9 r Chaptal
Berg, John ; 27 r la Bienfaisance
Bell, H. ; 30 r Faubourg St Honoré
Bird, Clarence A. ; 50 r Faubourg St. Denis
Bisbing, Henry ; 45 r Marché (Neuilly-sur-Seine)
Bissell, George ; 117 r Notre-Dame-des-Champs
Bixby, Eula, 9 ave McMahon

Blanc, E. H. ; 30 r Faubourg St. Honoré
Blackall, Clara ; 48 r de Lille
Blackman, Walter ; 28 r Pauquet
Blake, Mabel ; 7 r Galilée
Blashfield, E. H. ; 164 bd Haussmann
Blocki, Mr. ; Giez, near Fontainebleau
Blood, Flora ; 60 r Faubourg St. Denis
Boggs, F. M. ; 9 r Chaptal
Boit, Edward D. ; 32 ave Friedland
Borett, Elisabeth, 7 r Scribe
Boyden, Dwight F. ; 66 r de Seine
Boyle, John J. ; 255 bd d'Enfer
Boyle, Nellie E. ; 88 bd St. Michel
Breen, James ; 15 r Bray
Brewster, Amenda ; 7 r Galilée
Bride, Robert Louis ; Hotel d'Angleterre, r Jacob
Bridgman, F. A., Saturdays ; r Daubigny, (au bout)
Bridgman, George B. ; 65 r Madame
Brisbane, Alice ; 60 r Faubourg St. Denis
Bromley, F. B. ; 144 bd Malesherbes
Brown, C. M. ; 63 r de Seine
Brown, Walter J. ; 10 r des St. Pères
Browne, Mrs. Charles Gleason ; 10 r la Trémoille
Brownell, Franklin ; 14 r Navarin
Bunker, Dennis M. ; 16 bis r Gaieté
Bull, Alice ; 17 quai d'Orsay
Burnsley, J. M. ; 119 ave St. Germain des Puteaux
Bush-Brown, H. K. ; 255 bd d'Enfer
Butler, H. R. ; 147 r Villiers
Butler, T. E., 81 bd Montparnasse
Caldwell, Leslie ; 81 bd Montparnasse
Campbell, E. W. ; 17 ave Gourgaud
Carey, W. Astor ; 82 r d'Assas
Carl, Katherine A. ; 36 r Washington
Carrère, Jean ; 9 r Ecuries-d'Artois
Chadwick, Emma L. ; 7 r Scribe

Chadwick, F. B.; 13 r d'Aumale
Chamberlin, William; 3 r Tournon
Chambers, George W.; 120 ave Wagram
Clark, T. S.; address Drexell Harjes & Co.
Clarkson, R. E., 175 ave Victor-Hugo
Clements, G. H.; Vannes
Clienedienst, B. W.; 5 r Corneille
Cole, Adelaide; Hotel Balzac, r Balzac
Colin, M.; 28 r Faubourg St. Honoré
Conant, Lucy S.; 2 r Thénard; 30 r Faubourg St. Honoré
Collins, F. H.; r St. Placide
Coolidge, I. T.; 140 bd St. Germain
Copeland, Alfred B.; Hotel Brisson
Correja, Henry; 25 ave Villiers
Corryn, Henry; 23 r de Boulogne
Cox, Kenyon; 63 r de Seine
Crawford, Kenneth; 6 rue Mayet
Currier, Alger; 203 bd d'Enfer
Curtis, R. W.; 33 r Vaneau
Dana, C. E.; 13 r Washington
Dana, W. P. W., Saturdays; 75 r Courcelles
Danforth, Charles; 13 r Labie
Dannat, W. T., Saturdays; 71 ave Villiers
Davies, Charles H.; Fleury (Seine-et-Oise)
Day, Francis; 203 bd d'Enfer
Day, G. F.; 66 r de Seine
Denman, H. F.; in America
Dillon, H. P.; 84 bd Rochechouart
Dixwell, Anna; 50 r Faubourg St. Denis
Dodge, William; 3 r d'Alençon
Dodson, Sarah P. B.; 30 r Bassano
Dolph, J.; address Goupil & Co.
Donoghue, John; 188 r Vanves
Donoho, Ruger; 20 r Jacob
Dow, A. W.; Pont Aven, Finistère
Dubois, C. E.; 54 r des Saints-Pères

Dunbar, M. ; 7 r Douai
Durgin, Lyle ; 20 r Verneuil
Edwards, J. W. ; 147 ave Villiers
Emont, Anna de ; 28 r Faubourg St. Honoré
Evans, Miss ; 28 r Faubourg St. Honoré
Fairchild, Mary Louise ; passage des Panoramas
Fassitt, Francis Louis ; 20 r Mazarine
Felton, W. H. ; 13 r Duperré
Finn, J. H. ; 203 bd d'Enfer
Fish, Charles W. ; 78 r Taitbout
Fisher, J. R. ; 33 r Dauphine
FitzGerald A. ; Hotel Mirabeau
Flagg, H. P. ; 53 *bis* quai Grands-Augustins
Flagg, Montague ; 74 r de Seine
Flenner, J. W. ; 30 r Faubourg St. Honoré
Forbes, Charles S. ; 53 ave de l'Alma
Foster, J. H. ; 10 r la Tremoille
Fox, Mr. ; Ecole des Beaux-Arts
France, Jesse L. 220 bd d'Enfer
Furness, Rebecca F. ; 30 r Vaugirard
Gardner, Elisabeth J. ; 73 r Notre-Dame-des-Champs
Gardnier, Henry ; 65 r Saintonge .
Garrett, E. H. ; 140 ave Villiers
Gay, Walter ; 11 r Daubigny
Gibin, George ; 6 r Chartreuse
Gilman, B. F. ; 2 r Thénard
Godwin, B. ; 30 r Faubourg St. Honoré
Goodman, A. J. ; 3 r Bonaparte
Gray, Eliot ; 9 r des Beaux-Arts
Grayson, C. P. ; r Aumount-Thiéville
Gregory, Eliot ; in America
Gross, P. A. ; 7 r Chaptal
Guttierez, Carl ; 17 ave Gourgaud
Hale, Philip L. ; 13 r d'Alger
Hall, Ellen D. ; 2 r Thénard
Halle, H. W. ; 6 place l'Odéon

Hardie, R. S.; 71 ave Villiers
Harding, D. B. ; 35 r Marbeuf
Harrison, Alexander; 72 r Notre-Dame des Champs
Harwood, Bert; 33 bd d'Enfer
Hasbrouck, Mrs.; 6 r la Sorbonne
Hassam, Childe; 11 bd Clichy
Hastings, Thomas; 13 r l'Observatoire
Healy, G. P. A., Thursdays ; 64 r la Rochefoucauld
Heaton, A. G.; 155 r Faubourg St Honoré
Herrick, Miller; 7 r Lisbonne
Hewitt, Mrs. O.; 203 bd d'Enfer
    Hewitt, Miss
Hinckley, Robert; 54 r Notre-Dame-des-Champs
Hindeloper; 235 bd St. Germain
Hirschberg, Carl; 6 r des Chartreux
Hobbes, A. S.; 7 ave McMahon
Hoeber, Arthur; 21 rue Laffitte
Holman, Francis; 203 bd d'Enfer
Hopkins, T. M.; 30 r Faubourg St. Honoré
Howe, William H.; 157 ave Wagram
Howe, W. H.; 1 bis r Descombes
Huidekoper, Frank; 35, bd St. Germain
Hunt, Richard H.; 1 r Narbonne
Huppert, Edmund A.; 203 bd d'Enfer
Ives, Percy; 48 r d'Orsel
Jauregay, Esteban ; 20 r Mazarine
Jeançcon, Blanche; 59 r Sablons, Passy
Jewett, Mary; 12 bis r Descombes
Johnston, Samuel ; Cité du Retiro
Jones, F. C. ; 15 r Jacob
Joullin, Amédée; 48 r Faubourg St. Denis
Jurgensen, Louis O.; 3 r Bonaparte
Kavanagh, John ; 7 r Tournon
Kenyon, Henry ; 131 r St.
Ketson, A. H. ; 117 r Notre-Dame-des-Champs
Kindelberger, D. ; 30 r Faubourg St. Honoré

King, Emma C. ; 19 quai St. Michel
King, James S. ; 35 r de Seine
Kinselles, Katherine ; Passage des Panoramas
Klumpke, Anna ; 8 r de la Grande Chaumière
Klyn, Charles F. de ; 5 r Martin
Knight, D. R. ; place de l'Eglise, Poissy
Lamb, F. S. ; 39 r d'Orsel
Lancey, Ward de ; 145 ave Villiers
Lasar, Charles ; 47 r St. Placide
Larpenteur, James Desvarreaux ; 9 r Férou
Lasar, Charles F. ; 5 r Martin
Lash, L. W. ; 7 r de Tournoi
Lawrence, Nancy ; 48 r Faubourg St. Denis
Leighton, George W. ; 30 r Faubourg St. Honoré
Lesley, W. Margaret ; 2 r Thénard
Loomis, Chester ; 27 r Caulaincourt
Loomis, Eurilda ; 53 r Bonaparte
Loring, F. G.; 4 r San Paolo
Lucas, Albert ; 34 ave Trocadéro
Lucas, Miss ; 30 r Faubourg St. Honoré
Lucas, S. R.; 11 r Lord Byron
Mac Ewen, Walter ; address Meadows and Co., r Scribe
MacMonnies, F. W.; 11 imp du Maine
Mann, Julia ; 52 ave Kléber
Marcy, W. L.; 164 bd Montparnasse
Mathews, Arthur F.; 12 r de Seine
Maybeck ; 71 r de Rennes
Mayor, Ernest ; 35 bd des Capucines
McDougall, J. A., jr.; 9 r de l'Orient, Montmartre
McDowell, E. W.; 6 r des Chartreux
Melchers, Julius Gari ; 27 r Tournon
Michaels, H. Burr ; 34 ave Trocadéro
Middleton, Stanley ; 34 ave Trocadéro
Miles, J. R.; 66 r de Seine
Mills, Harry ; 29 r Laval
Mitchell, Mrs.; 30 r Faubourg St. Honoré

Monks, R. H.; address Munroe and Co.

Morse, Alice; passage des Panoramas

Morse, W. P.; 10 r Croix des Petits Champs

Mosler, Henry, Saturdays; 12 r la Tremoille

Moss, C. E.; 34 r Fontaine St. Georges

Moss, Frank; 13 r Laval

Mowbray, H. S.; 7 r Tourlagne

Munsell, A. H. ; 3 r Mayran

Nettleton, Walter, 33 r Jacob

Newman, B. T. ; 20 bd d'Enfer

Newmann, Carl ; Hotel d'Angleterre, r Jacob

Newmann, Henry ; 8 r St. Georges

Nugent, J. M. ; 3 r Bonaparte

O'Halloran, J. J. ; 2 r Odessa

Osgood, Miss W. K. ; 36 r St. Ferdinand

Page, W. G.; 66 r de Seine

Parker, Stephan Hills, Saturdays ; 64 r la Rochefoucauld

Parshall, de Witt ; 7 r Tournon

Patrick, John Douglas ; 13 r Duperré

Pearce, Charles Sprague ; Anvers (Seine-et-Oise)

Peel, Paul ; 11 r l'Ancienne-Comédie

Peirce, H. Winthrop ; 8 r de Navarin

Penfold, F. C. ; Port Aven (Finistère)

Pennie, R. M. ; 14 r de Navarin

Pennington, R. G. H. ; 15 r Boissonnade

Peters, Clinton ; 4 r Luxembourg

Peters, C. R. ; 7 r Tournon

Potter, Edward C. ; 15 r Campagne Première

Poucher, W. E. ; address Munroe & Co.

Prichard, J. ; 28 r Faubourg St Honoré

Raught, John ; 66 r de Seine

Reid, R. L.; 24 r Jacob

Reinhart, A. G. ; 147 ave Villiers

Reinhart, C. S. ; 147 ave Villiers

Rich, Thomas P. ; 55 r la Grande-Chaumière

Richardson, Frank H.; 10 r Croix-des-Petits-Champs

Rhees, M. G. ; 33 r Tournon
Robbins, Lucy Lee ; 17 quai d'Orsay
Ryder, Henry O. ; 57 r de Lille
Ruckstuhl, F. W. ; 203 bd d'Enfer
Santry, Daniel François ; 15 r Jacob
Sargent, J. S. ; London (England)
Sass, George ; 66 r Notre-Dame-des-Champs
Scott, E. M. ; 7 r Scribe
Seawell, Nancy ; passage des Panoramas
Shean, Charles M. ; 49 r Denfert-Rochereau
Shonborn, J. L. ; Montleveque (*près* Senlis)
Simmons, E. E. ; 7 r Scribe
Simmons, F. W. ; 7 r Tournon
Simmons, Vesta S. ; 7 r Scribe
Simons, Marius ; 18 r du Bois-de-Boulogne
Singer, Winnaretta ; 77 r Amsterdam
Slade, Emily ; 53 ave d'Iena
Small, Frank Otis ; 54 r Lamartine
Smedley, V. N. ; 3 r Bonaparte
Smith, de Cost ; 38 r Ramey
Smith, A. P. ; Pont Aven, Finistère
Smith, E. B. ; 5 r Douai
Smith, John Lewis ; r Fontaine-St.-George
Smith, Sarah.Ida ; 36 r St.-Ferdinand
Snow, Clara ; 59 ave Kléber
Soneel, Louis ; 3 r du Bac
Spencer, Charles ; 70 *bis* r Notre-Dame-des-Champs
Springer, Eva ; 59 ave Kléber
Stark, Otto ; 6 r Chapelais
Sterner, Albert E. ; 29 r Laval
Stevens Miss ; 13 r Châteaubriand
Stewart, J. L. ; 36 r Copernic
Stokes, F. W. ; 81 bd Montparnasse
Stone, George M. 129 r Sèvres
Stone, William ; 24 r Jacob
Story, Julian ; 7 r place des Etats Unis

Strain, Daniel ; 19 r Clauzel
Strickland, Charles Hobart ; 36 ave d'Iena
Strong, Elizabeth ; 3 r des Saints Pères
Sturgess, Mrs. ; 99 ave Champs-Elysées
Taylor, L. C. ; 7 r Scribe
Thaw, Mrs.; 8 r la Grand-Chaumière
Thaxter, Percy ; 2 r Thénard
Theriat, C. J.; 83 ave Marceau
Tojetti, Virgil ; 5 r Pelouse
Tompkins, Clementina ; 11 bd de Clichy
Trotter, Miss ; passage des Panoramas
Truesdell, G. S. ; 3 r Campagne-Première
Tuckerman, Arthur L. ; 18 ave Kléber
Tuke, H. S. ; 2 r Odessa
Uhl, Jerome ; 17 r Notre-Dame-des-Champs
Vail, Eugene L. ; 34 ave Trocadéro
Vanderpoel, John H. ; 3 r Bonaparte
Vonnoh, Robert ; r Croix-des-Petits-Champs
Voss, E. C. ; 5 r Saussaies
Walden, Lionel ; 18 *bis* imp du Maine
Walkeley, B. D. ; 87 r Rochechouart
Weeks, E. L. ; 128 ave Wagram
Wewardson, John ; 20 r Mazarine
Whidden, William ; 83 r du Bac
Whistler, James McNiel ; 13 r Dragon
Whiteman, J. Edwin ; 8 r St. Hyacinthe-St. Honoré
Wickenden, R. J.; 9 r de l'Université
Wight, M. ; 49 bd Rochechouart
Williams, Elisabeth ; 59 r Vaugirard
Williams, F. D. ; 35 *bis* r de Fleurus
Williams, Mrs. L. L. ; 54 r Logier
Wilson, Edmond Russell; 83 r du Bac
Wolff, Otto ; 5 r Laval
Wood, Ogden ; 9 r Bochard-de-Sarron
Woodward, Mr. ; 48 r Faubourg St. Denis
Wright, Frederick ; 12 r Boissonade

Wüertz, Emil; 1 r l'Ambre
Yelland, R. D. ; 141 bd St. Michel
Zogbaum, Miss ; r Brochand, (Batignolles)

AMERICAN PICTURES AT THE SALON SINCE 1808.

The original intention of including in this list the pictures exhibited at the universal expositions was abandoned because of numerous repetitions. The standard of admission was much lower in these cases nearly everything that was sent having been accepted almost without question. The omissions aside from these have been caused by inability to find the catalogue needed at the National Library, or the fact that some few names among so many have been overlooked. Sketches have not in every case been included. The list as it stands is sufficiently voluminous, and it has the commanding merit of being an epitome of American art representing, with the exception of the masters of the revolutionary period, its origin and gradual expansion both at home and abroad. The first American artist who exhibited at the Salon found himself in excellent company. It is therefore the more remarkable that he should have been distinguished with a medal. The exhibition at the Musée Napoléon in 1808 comprised over five hundred works of art and the catalogue which has not even yet become a book of surpassing beauty, is a queer little old-fashioned 32-mo. volume curious in binding, quaint in typography and naive in its explanations and general phraseology. When the labor necessary for the preparation of the present list is considered its errors will appear few and trivial.

1808.—Vanderlyn, John, *Caius Marius among the Ruins of Carthage.*

1836.—Healy, G. P. A., *Full-length Portrait of a Gentleman. Portrait of a Gentleman.*

1837.—Healy, G. P. A., *Family Portraits.*

1838.—Healy, Thomas C., *Portrait of a Gentleman.*

1839.—Healy, G. P. A., *Portrait of General Cass.*

1840.—Healy, G. P. A., *Portrait of Mrs. Lewis Cass.*

1841.—Healy, G. P. A., *Portrait of Marshal Soult. Portrait of a Gentleman. Portrait of Dr. Brewster. Portrait of Two Young Ladies.* Vanderlyn, John, *Niagara Falls.*

1842.—Healy, G. P. A., *The Two Sisters. Portrait of a Young Lady.* Tanner, A. Wilson, *Low Tide on the Normandy Coast.*

1844.—Healy, G. P. A., *Eight Portraits.*

1845.—Healy, G. P. A., *Portrait of Louis Philippe. Portrait of the United States Minister. Portrait of a Young Gentleman.* Vanderlyn, John, *Portrait of a Gentleman.*

1847.—Nahl, Charles, *Otto of Wittelsbach.*

1848.—Bethune, Henry, *Banks of the Orne. Banks of the Moselle. Forest of Fontainebleau. Landscape.* Brown, G. L., *Fisherman's Island (Lago Maggiore). Lorenzo and Jessica.* Jackson, William, *Bacchus and Love. Portrait.* Nahl, Charles, *Death of Bayard.*

1850.—Healy, G. P. A., *Portrait of Louis Philippe. Portrait of John C. Calhoun. Portrait of a Lady. Portrait of a Lady and Child. Portrait of Mrs. Liesieur, of Norfolk, Va. Portrait of Dr. Oliff. Portrait of a son of Mr. Corbin. Portrait.*

1852.—Hunt, William, *Good Luck. Marguerite.*

1853.—Ehringer, John William, *Yankee Peddler.* Hunt, William Morris, *Study.* Mezzara, Joseph, *Portrait of a Young Lady. Portrait of a Gentleman.*

1855.— (General Exposition). Babcock exhibited 8 pictures, Cranch 2, Gignoux 4, Healy 14, Hunt (H. P.) 1, Hunt (W. M.) 3, Powers 2, Robertson 1, Rossiter 3, Walcutt 1, Greenough and Warburg exhibited pieces of sculpture.

1857.—Cranch, C. P., *View on the Hudson. Autumn Sunset. Forest of Fontainebleau. Bas Bréau, Forest of Fontainebleau.* May, Edward H., *Neapolitan Shepherd. Portrait of a Young Lady.*

1859.—Faxon, Richard, *Regatta at Royan, near Verdon, Mouth of the Gironde).* May, Edward H., *Francis First Lamenting the Death of his Son. Haidee and Zoe finding the Body of Don Juan on the Beach. Italian Peasant writing the Confession of his Love on a Tomb. Portrait of a Lady.* Rothermel, P. F., *Saint Agnes. Giants' Staircase, Venice. The Virtuoso.* Sculpture.—Greenough, Richard, *Equestrian statue of Washington. Indian Pursued by Civilization* (statuette in plaster).

1861.—Dana, W. P., *Cour de Ferme à Etretat.* Faxon, Richard, *Ship Lying to.* May, Edward H., *Last Days of Christopher Columbus. Dispute between the Baron Bradwardine and Balmanhapph. Portrait of Jerome Bonaparte. Portrait of a Lady. Portrait of a Young Lady.*

1863.—May, Edward H., *The Jews at Babylon. Lady Jane Grey going to Execution. The Toilet.* Sculpture.—Greenough, Richard, *Portrait of Motley* (bust in marble). Mezzara, Joseph P., *Bust in Marble.*

1864.—Langdon, Woodbury, *Banks of Lake Leman. Coast of Normandy.*

May, Edward H., *Portrait of Mr. Dayton, American Minister at Paris.* Tait, John R., *Lake of the Four Cantons.*

1865.—Babcock, W. P., *Girl and Squirrel.* Faxon, Richard, *Sunset on the Garonne. Barque.* Langdon, Woodbury, *The Storm. Sunset.* Marshall, William R., *Portrait of a Gentleman.* May, Edward H., *Portrait of a Gentleman.* Mayer, Francis B., *The Crazy Philosopher. The Lost Letter.* Thompson, Alfred W., *Brushwood Thicket at Ebu Fargis.* Welsh, Theodore Charles, *Temple of Paestum. Lago Maggiore.* Whistler, James McNiel, *Princess of the Land of Porcelain.*

1866.—Babcock, W. P., *Children Bathing. Flowers.* Durand, Charles, *Hercules at the feet of Omphale.* Faxon, Richard, *Fontarabia. Boat in a Squall.* Langdon, Woodbury, *Seashore. At Sea.* May, Edward H., *Amy Robsart and the Colporteur. Portrait.* Mayer, Francis B., *The May Festival* (Indian scene). Robertson, J. Roy, *Portrait of Sir Henry de Houghton.* Ware, John, *The Little Mill at Cernay. Huts of Irish Squatters* (N.Y.)

1867.—Bacon, Henry, *Snow Effect.* Butler, George, *Newfoundland Dog.* Faxon, Richard, *Ocean Steamer leaving Bordeaux.* Haseltine, William Stanley, *Capri. Cliffs at Capri.* Hunt, William, *Portrait of a Gentleman. Portrait of a Lady.* Moran, Thomas, *American Forest.* Owen, George, *American Scene.* Whistler, James McNiel, *At the Piano. Winter on the Thames.*

1868.—Bacon, Henry, *The First Visit. The Braconniers* (snow effect). Bridgman, Frederick A., *Breton Game.* Gardner, E. J. *The Three Friends. Still Life.* Haldeman, E. J., *At Ecouen* (Seine-et-Oise). Lewis, John S., *La Pêche Perdue.* May, E. H., *Ophelia. The Reading.* Ramsey, Milne, *Beer and Tobacco* (still life). Stevenson, Mary, *The Mandoline.* Tiffany, Louis, *Still Life.* Ware, John, *Court at Marlotte. Beach at Villerville.*

1869.—Bacon, Henry, *Lost Money. Where is Mother ?* Bridgman, F. A., *Carnival in Brittany. The Pet Pigeon.* Dubois, C. E., *After the Rain* (Lake of the Four Cantons). Gardner, E. J., *Return from the Chase.* Healy, G. P. A., *Portrait of General Grant.* Johnson, Samuel F., *Interior. Apples.* Loop, Mrs., *Portrait.* May, E. H. *Portrait of Anson Burlingame. Portrait of a Lady.* Owen, George, *Hill of Sannois. The Seine near Argenteuil.* Ramsey, Milne, *Jewels* (still life). Ware, John, *Beach and Cliff* (Dournenez, Finistère). Wilson, Esther, *Portrait of General Grant.* Sculpture.—Mezzara, Joseph, *Portrait* (bust in marble).

1870.—Babcock, W. P., *Le Chaperon Rouge. The Bird's Nest.* Bacon, Henry, *Paying the Bill. The Friends,* Bridgman, Frederick A., *Un Cirque en Province. What are the Girls Talking About ?* Chapman C., *Mexican Valley. Beach at Trouville.* Lewis, John S., *Study.* May, Edward H., *Arviragus bearing off the body of Cymbeline.* Ryder, D. Platt, *Italian Page.* Sachs, Jules, *The Rat which had withdrawn from the World* (Fontaine). Smith, Frank H., *Breton Servant. Evening in Finistère.* Stevenson, Mary, *A Contadina* (Piedmont). Swift Clement, *A Court.* Tuckerman, Ernest, *Playthings.* Ware, John, *Banks of the Seine near Meulan.* Welch, Thomas B., *Portrait of J. C. Calhoun. Portrait of General Johnston.* Wilson, Hester, *Portrait.* Wylie, Robert, *" Baz Waten."* Sculpture.— Mezzara, Joseph, *Portrait* (bust in marble).

1872.—Bacon, Henry, *Avenue Montaigne.*—Baird, W. B., *Return of the Prisoner.* Bridgman, Frederick A., *Apollo carrying off Cyrene. A Lande in Brittany.* Dana, W. P. W., *Extremes Meet* (New York). *Bay of Saint Brelades* (Jersey). Dubois, Charles E., *Forest of Fontainebleau* (September).

In the Forest of Fontainebleau. Gardner, E. J., *Cinderella.* Healy, G. P. A., *Portrait of a Lady.* May, E. H., *Portrait of John M. Read, U. S. Consul.* Stevenson, Mary, *During the Carnival.* Swift, Clement, *Spring in Lower Brittany. Souvenirs of Lower Brittany.* Wylie, Robert, *The Breton Sorceress.*

1873.—Bacon, Henry, *The Choice* (Alsace). Bridgman, Frederick A. *Moorish Interior. La Rentrée du Maïs* (Basses-Pyrénées). Dubois, Charles E., *Swiss Cottages. Auvernier. Lake Neuchatel.* Knight, Daniel Rridgway, *The Fugitives.* Lewis, John J. S., *Old Woman.* May, Edward H., *The Magdalen at the Tomb. Portrait of Lieutenant de Kodolitsch, Attaché of Austrian Embassy.* Richards, William T., *In the Forest* (winter effect). Tompkins, Clementina, *Portrait of a Lady. Portrait of a Lady.* Tuckerman, Ernest, *Tomb of Sidi Abder Rhaman at Algiers.* Wylie, Robert, *The Orphan's Welcome* (Brittany). *Sleep.*

1874.—Babcock, W. P., *The Gorges of Rochefort, Fontainebleau,* Baird, William, *Mother of the Family.* Bridgman, Frederick A., *In the Pyrenees.* Gardner, Elisabeth Jane, *Corinne. Jeannie and Blanche.* Inness, George, *Environs of Perugia* (Italy). Lafarge, John, *Valley of the Last* (Newport. R. J.) Lewis, J. S., *Portrait of a Lady.* May, Edward H., *End of the Reading. Souvenir of the Commune.* Swift, Clement, *Souvenir of Finistère.* Yewel, George Henry, *Senate Hall of the Ducal Palace at Venice.* Stevens, Carles W., *Portrait of a Lady* (aquarelle). Sculpture.—Bartlett, T. H., *The Child and the Shell* (statuette in bronze).

1875.—Bacon, Henry, *The Boys of Boston Complaining to General Gage.* Bierstadt, Albert, *Sunset on the Prairies.* Blashfield, E. H., *A Young Poet.* Bridgman, Frederick A., *A Still Day in Upper Egypt. The Nubian Story-teller in the Harem.* Brown, J. Appleton, *Summer. The Seashore at Dives* (Calvados). Cole, J. Foxcroft, *Pasture in Normandy.* Volk, Stephen A. G., *In Brittany.* Eakin, Thomas, *Hunting Scene.* Gardner, Elisabeth Jane, *The Sorceress.* Healy, G. P. A., *Portrait of Miss J. Bryant. Portrait of Lord Lyons. Portrait of Dr. T. W. Evans.* Knight, D. R. *The Washerwomen.* Leland, Henry, *Portrait of a Gentleman.* May, Edward H., *Portrait of General Carroll Tevis. Portrait of Dr. Piorry, of the Academy of Medicine.* Sartain, Emily, *Portrait of a Young Lady. La Pièce à Conviction.* Swift, *Bon Voyage. Le Braconnier.* Tompkins, Clementina, *An Artist's Début.* Walker, J. A., *The Field of Battle. A Védette.* Wylie, Robert, *A Colporteur. Ragpicker and Seller of Faience* (Finistère). Sculpture.—Mezzara, Joseph, *Portrait of a Lady* (bust in marble).

1876.—Anderson, A. A., *Young Oriental.* Bacon, Henry, *Franklin at Home.* Baird, William, *Forest of Fontainebleau. Hen and Chickens.* Blashfield, Edwin H., *The Toreador. My Lord.* Bolt, E. D., *Beach at Villers* (Calvados). Bridgman, Frederick A., *The Faithful at Prayer* (mosque at Cairo). *Departure of the Holy Carpet* (Cairo). Bunce, W. G., *Evening at Venice.* Dubois, C. E., *Windmill near Dordrecht, Holland.* Healy, G. P. A., *Portrait of Cardinal McCloskey. Portrait of Liszt.* Knight, D. R., *Harvest Feast.* Leland, Henry, *Portrait of a Young Lady.* Lippincott, W. H., *Portrait of a Gentleman.* May, E. H., *Portrait of a Young Lady. An Alsatian Woman.* Parker, S. H., *Portrait of a Lady.* Pearce, Charles Sprague, *Portrait of a Young Lady.* Picknell, W. L., *A Breton Farm.* Ramsey, Milne, *The Naturalist.* Ward, E. M., *Au Lavoir* (Finistère). *The Sabot-maker.* Sketches, etc.—Bigelow, William, *The Loges de Raphael at the Vatican* (aquarelle). Sculpture.—Bartlett, T. H., *Episode of the War of Rebellion* (group in bronze).

1877.—Anderson, A. A., *Portrait of a Lady.* Bacon, Henry, *At Sea* (steamship Pereire). Baird, William B., *A Road at Clamart* (Seine-et-Oise). Beackman, Walter, *The Son's Farewell.* Blashfield, E. H., *A Roman Augur.* Bloomer, H. R., *After the Storm. Landscape.* Bolton, H. Jones, *Road in Brittany.* Bridgman, Frederick A., *A Mummy's Funeral.* Cole, J. Foxcroft, *Landscape with animals* (Calvados). Coleman, C. C., *The Horses of St. Mark.* Copeland, Alfred Bryant, *A Dutch Interior after Stein.* Dana, W. P. W., *Dinard Beach at Low Tide* (Ile-et-Vilaine). Dodson, Sarah P. B., *L'Amour Ménétrier.* Dubois, Charles E., *The Hudson near West Point. Evening.* Gardner, Elisabeth J., *Ruth and Naomi.* Healy, G. P. A., *Portrait of Gambetta. Portrait of a Young Lady.* Johnson, David, *On the Housatonic.* Knight, Daniel R., *Village Water-Carriers.* Loomis, Chester, *Une Bonne Pipe.* Low, Will Hickok, *Portrait of Albani. Le Jour des Morts* (plaine de Barbizon). May, Edward H., *Antonia, Portrait of a Gentleman.* Middleton, Stanley, *At Honfleur.* Moss, Frank, *The Sibyl.* Pearce, Charles Sprague, *Portrait of a Young Lady. Death of the First Born.* Sargent, John S., *Portrait of a Young Lady.* Swift, Clement, *Wreckers.* Thayer, Abbot H., *Sleep.* Tompkins, Clementina, *Rosa, the Spinner.* Ward, Myron, *Portrait of a Lady. Portrait of a Gentleman.* Sketches, etc.—Boit, Edward D., *Porta del Popolo, Rome* (aquarelle).

1878.—Babcock, W. P., *Rochefort. Fontainebleau.* Bacon, H., *The Adieux.* Baird, W. B., *Bois de Clamart* (Seine). *Springtime.* Blackman, Walter, *News from the City. What, Already ?* Blashfield, E. H., *The Emperor Commodus Leaving the Amphitheater.* Bloomer, H. Reynolds, *A Waterfall in Seine-et-Oise.* Brandegee, Robert B., *Portrait.* Bridgman, Frederick A., *Divertissement of a Syrian King. Portrait of a Lady.* Bunce, W. G., *Morning in Venice. Evening in Venice.* Bunner, A. F., *The Fisher's Hut.* Chase, Henry, *English Fishermen.* Coleman, Charles C., *Appletree Branches in Bloom.* Copeland, Alfred Bryant, *Interior of St. Jacques, Antwerp.* Crowninshield, Frederick, *L'Enfance, la Sévérité, la Douceur Maternelle.* Dana, William P. W., *Gathering Seaweed.* Davis, John, *Indian Chief. Big Dog.* Dubois, Charles Edward, *Morning in the Meadow.* Dunsmore, J. W., *A Revery.* Eaton, Charles Frederick, *Portrait.* Fowler Frank, *The Ancient Fountain.* Gardner, Elisabeth Jane, *Moses in the Bulrushes.* Healy, G. P. A., *Portrait of General Grant. Portrait of a Young Lady.* Lippincott, W. H., *Portrait of a Young Lady.* May, Edward H., *Susannah's Dream. Portrait of General Torbert.* Middleton, Stanley, *The Chase* (in Yonne). Moran, Edward, *Morning after the Storm* (Bay of Biscay). Mosler, Henry, *Sorrows of Infancy. The Quadroon Slave.* Parker, Stephen Hills, *Nouvelles à la Main.* Perkins, J. C., *La Religieuse.* Picknell, N. L., *A Lande in Finistère.* Ramsey, Milne, *Cromwell and his Daughter Elisabeth.* Ruff, Margaret, *Still Life.* Smith, Calvin Ray, *Une Petite Italienne.* Stewart, Jules L., *La Maja. The Reading.* Swift, Clement, *Load of Seaweed* (on the beach, Brittany). Thayer, Abbot A., *Portrait.* Tojetti, Domenico, *Venus and Cupid.* Ward, Edgar Melville, *Paternal Pride. A Venice Street.* Ward, de Lancey, *Study of a Female Head.* Weeks, E. L., *A Moorish Camel Drive* (Tangiers). Sketches, etc.—Copeland, A. B., *Havre Harbor.* Darwill, Corinne, *Rebecca* (copy). Greenough, Gordon, *Portrait.* Stone, Mary L., *Grandfather's Trunk* (aquarelle). Ward, de Lancey, *Man of the People, Rome* (pastel). Sculpture.—Bartlett, T. H., *Lincoln* (statuette in plaster). *Oakes Ames* (statuette in plaster).

1879.—Anderson, A. A., *David Keeping his Father's Sheep.* Bacon, Henry, *Burial at Sea.* Baird, William B., *At Grez* (Seine-et-Marne). Baker, Ellen B.,

Portrait of a Lady. Bispham, C. H., *Sultan.* Blashfield, Edwin H., *Roman Ladies at the School of Gladiators.* Brandegee, Robert B., *Portrait.* Bridgman, Frederick A., *Procession of the Ox Apis.* Bunce, William G., *Morning at Venice.* Chase, Henry, *Dutch Fishermen* (at Sheveningen). Coffin, William A., *Inn in Brittany. An Academy of Modern Painting.* Conant, Cornelia, *Family Life.* Cox, Warren, *Young Venice Girl.* Dana, William P. W., *Les Brisants.* Daniel, George, *Winter Effect* (Forest of Fontainebleau). *Oranges and Apples.* Dodson, Sarah P. B., *Deborah. The Dance.* Dubois, Charles E. *October, Swiss Hut at foot of Mount Vuilly.* Flagg, Montague, *Portrait.* Gardner, E. J., *At the Fountain.* Gay, Walter, *The Fencing Lesson. Landscape* (Fontainebleau). Greatorex, Kathleen, *Flowers of Mentone.* Hyneman, H. N., *Desdemona.* Healy, G. P. A., *Two Portraits of Ladies.* Heaton, A. G., *A Little Calculation. A Special Favor.* Hlasko, Anna, *Portrait.* Irwin, Benoni, *The Rivals. Portrait of a Young Lady.* Jones, H. Bolton, *End of the Day.* Knight, Daniel R. *The Vintage.* Lippincott, William H., *A Day of Leave.* Loomis, Chester, *Viola* (from "Twelfth Night".) May, Edward H., *Portrait of a Lady. Curiosity.* Maynard, G. W., *Portrait of a Gentleman.* Mosler, Henry, *The Return. Les Femmes et le Secret.* Parker, Stephen Hills, *St. Sebastian after his Punishment eared for by the Christians.* Pattison, J. W., *Two Children.* Pearce, C. S., *Abraham's Sacrifice.* Perkins, F. A., *An Italian.* Picknell, W. L., *Valley of the Rustine.* Ramsey, Milne, *Presentation of a Lettre de Cachet.* Sargent, John S., *Portrait of Carolus Duran. In the Olives at Capri.* Shonborn, Lewis J., *Portrait of a Gentleman.* Stewart, Jules L., *Portrait of a Lady.* Stone, Mary L. *The Angelus.* Swift, Clément, *A Wreck.* Tojetti, Domenico, *Elaine. Francesca de Rimini.* Torrev, Eugene, *L'Annonce.* Ward, Edgar Melville, *The Cooper.* Ward, de Lancey, *Un Savetier Italien.* Williams, Frederick D., *Street at Montigny.* Woodward, W. W., *A Cour in Old Paris.* Sketches, etc.—Boit, Edward Darley, *St. Peter's in Rome* (water color). *Mont St. Michel* (water color). Faller, Emily, *Portrait of a Young Lady on Porcelaine.* Greenough, Gordon, *Study.* Hardie, Robert G., *Portrait in Crayon.* Merrill, Emma F. R. *The Little Sister* (after Greuze). Walker, Sophia A., *Portrait of a Young Lady.*

1880.—Bacon, Henry, *Flirtation Behind the Wheelhouse.* Baird, William, *Cows. Sheep.* Baker, Ellen K., *Street Merchant. Dolce far Niente.* Beckwith, Arthur, *Jeanne d'Arc at Orleans. King Midas' Wish.* Bispham, H. C., *Valley of the Var near Nice.* Blackman, Walter, *Un Jeu de Quilles. Jealousy.* Blashfield, Edwin H., *Besieged Welcoming their Deliverers.* Boggs, Frank Myers, *Rue d'Alleray* (Vaugirard). Bolter, J., *Near Tangiers* (Morocco). Bridgman, F. A., *Arab House at Biskra. Tents of Nomads at Biskra.* Brown, Walter Francis, *Old Bridge at Gretz. Gretz-sur-Loing.* Coffin, William Anderson, *Mandolin Player. Sire John.* Copeland, Alfred Bryants, *The Artist's Garret.* Cox, Kenyon, *Lady in Black. In the Grass.* Daniel, George, *Village in the Eastern Pyrenees. Valley of the Vernet.* Davis, John Steeple, *Portrait of Horace Greeley.* Delprat, J. S., *Golden Pheasants.* Dubois, Charles Edward, *Autumn Evening on Lake Neufchâtel.* Flagg, Charles V., *Portrait.* Gardner, Elisabeth Jane, *Priscilla. The Water's Edge.* Gay, Walter, *Les Pigeons Savants. Les Amateurs de Fleurs.* Gregory, Eliot, *Portrait. A Soubrette.* Harrison, Alexander, *Breton Coast.* Healy, G. P. A., *Portrait of Emma Thursby. Portrait of a Lady.* Heaton, Augustus G., *Baths at Trouville. A Bather.* Hilliard, William Henry, *Moorish House at Algiers. Arab Cemetery* (Algiers). Hinckley, Robert, *Pygmalion.* Knight, Daniel Ridgeway, *A Halt.* Lancey, Ward de, *The Good-for-Nothing.* Lippincott, William H., *Portrait of a Gentleman.* Mason, Louis Gage, *Florentine Study.* May, Edward H., *Saint Magdalen at the Sepulcher. The Song.* Morgan, Charles W., *Peasant Woman.* Mosler, Henry, *The Wedding Dress. The Spinner.* Moss, Charles E., *Italian Girl.* Nicholls, Burr H., *Le Vieux Foyer.* Parker, Stephen Hills, *Portrait of a Gentleman. Portrait of a Young Lady.* Perkins, F. A., *Portrait of a Young Lady.* Picknell, W. L., *The Edge of the Marsh. Route of Concarneau.* Reilly, John Lewis, *Portrait of a Gentleman.* Sargent, John S., *Portrait of a Lady. Smoke of Ambergris.* Shonborn, Lewis J., *Stable Interior.* Stone, Maria L., *Children of the Village.* Strain, Daniel, *Portrait of a Lady.* Swift, Clement, *Finishing the Load.* Tuckerman, Ernest, *Interior of Knols Castle.* Walker, Henry, *The Philter.* Weeks, Edwin, *Embarking Camels* (Morocco). *Part of Ancient Fondah* (Morocco). Williams, Frederick D., *Mill at Cernay-la-Ville. Mill.* Woodward, Wilbur Winfield, *Ossian.* Wright, Marian Lois, *A Venetian Gondolier.* **Sketches, etc.**—Berend, Edward, *Young Girl.* Boker, Orleana von Weissenfels. *Portrait* (faience). Chauncey, Lucy, *Portrait of a Young Lady* (on porcelaine). *Les Ennuyés* (faience). Clark, George, *Four Aquarelles.* Crocker, Sallie S., *Portland, U.S. Portrait.* Dana, Charles E., *Mont St. Michel* (aquarelle). *Gate of Justice, Alhambra* (aquarelle). Dixey, Ellen S., *Moorish House, Algiers.* Denohoe, Eliza, *Portrait on Porcelain.* Goodridge, S. M., *Two Portraits.* Greatorex, Eleanor, *Mère Elisabeth* (at Hotel Cluny). Greatorex, Kathleen, *Two Flower Pieces.* Hardie, Robert G., *Portrait of a Lady* (in crayon). Merrill, Emma F. R., *Two Portraits.* Mezzara, Rosina, *Portrait* (enamel). Pattison, William J., *In the Meadow* (water-color). Tompkins, Clementina, *Portrait.* Walker, Sophia A., *Portrait.* Wheeler, Mary C., *Study of a Horse's Head.* Whidden, Mary William, *Bathroom* (Alhambra). *Puerta del Vino* (Alhambra). **Sculpture.**—Bartlett, Paul Wayland, *Old Woman* (bust in plaster). Ezekiel, Moses. *Faith* (figure in plaster). *Portrait* (bust in marble). Mezzara, Joseph, *Pierre Landrey* (bust in marble)

1881.—Baird, William, *Herd in the South of France. Returning from Pasture.* Barse, George Rudolph, *Portrait.* Blackman, Walter, *The Peace of Evening.* Boggs, Frank Myers, *Déchargement du Crabier* (Dieppe). *Fishing Boat* (Dieppe). Boit, Edward Darley, *Pine Parasols* (Cannes). Bolton, Jones, *Winter at New York.* Bromwell, Frank, *Abel.* Brown, Walter Francis, *Corner at Etretat.* Chadwick, Francis Brooks, *Study.* Chase, William M., *A Smoker.* Copeland, Alfred Bryant, *Interior of the Maison Hydraulique, Anvers.* Curtis, Ralph Wormeley, *Venice.* Dana, William P. W., *Fishing Boat in Heavy Weather. Un Grain.* Daniel, George, *Gorge in the Pyrenees.* Davis, Charles H., *Forest, Fontainebleau.* Desvarreaux, James Larpenteur, *Pasture in the Valley of Argelès.* Dillon, Henry, *Bouquet-Selle.* Donoho, Gaines R., *Edge of the Forest.* Dubois, Charles Edward, *Morning in August.* Duveneck, T., *Portrait of a Lady.* Flagg, Montague, *Portrait of a Gentleman.* Gardner, Elisabeth, *In a Strange Land.* Gay, Walter, *Les Ennuis du Célibat. Souvenir of Spain.* Grayson, Clifford P., *Breton Idyl.* Greatorex, Kathleen, *Head of an Arab.* Harrison, Alexander, *Shipwreck. Seashore.* Harrison, Birge, *Une Epave.* Healy, G. P. A., *Portrait of de Lesseps. Portrait of the King of Roumania.* Hilliard, William Henry, *Isle of Jersey.* Hinckley, Robert, *Last Moments of Socrates. Portrait of a Young Lady.* Knight, Daniel Bridgway, *After Breakfast* (by the Seine). Lancey, William Ward, *Portrait of a Lady.* Lippincott, William H., *Portrait of Young Lady. Two Good Friends.* Mason, Lewis Gage, *Study.* May, Edward Harrison, *Portrait of Lord Conyers. La Levée de Mademoiselle.* Mosler, Henry, *Eve of the Battle. Return from Fishing.* Moss, Charles E. *The Prodigal Son.* Moss, Frank, *Christ and the Doctors.* Murdoch, C. R., *The Barrier.* Natt, Phœbe, *Head of a Moor.* Nicholls, Burr H., *The Cabbage-seller.* Parker, Stephen H.,

Portrait of a Gentleman. The Bohemienne. Pearce, Charles S., *Beheading of John the Baptist* (Decollation). Picknell, W. L., *Landscape.* Sargent, John S., *Three Portraits.* Shonborn, Lewis J., *Clearing off the Brush. Jean de Grès.* Simmons, Edward E., *Portrait.* Strain, Daniel, *The Two Friends. Study.* Swift, Clement, *Dragueurs de Sable.* Tryon, William D., *Harvest in Picardy. On the Meuse.* Weeks, Edwin L., *Camels at the Cistern.* Williams, L. L., *A Friendly Circle.* Wolff, Otto, *Portrait of a Young Gentleman.* **Sketches. etc.**--Bowlend, George B., *Will-o-the Wisp* (aquarelle). Croker, Sallie S., *Portrait on Wood.* Dana, Charles E., *Farm at Etretat* (aquarelle). Jilton, Alice, *Bluets* (water color). Mezzara, Rosina, *Two Enamels* (émaux) Sargent, John S., *Two Venice Views.* Slocomb, Cora, *A Young Lady of Baltimore.* Tompkins, Clementina, *Head of an Italian Woman.* Van, Louisa, *Portrait on Porcelaine.* **Sculpture.**—Bartlett, Paul W., *Dog's Head* (bronze). Ezekiel, Moses, *Judith* (bust in marble). *Young Man* (bust in bronze). Phinney, Emma Elizabeth, *Negro's Head* (bust in bronze). Walz, John, *Portrait in Plaster* (medallion). Warner, Olin, *Portrait* (bust in bronze).

1882.—Allen, Thomas, *Evening on the Square* (San Antonio, Texas). Bacon, Henry, *The Sailor's Story.* Bierstadt, *American Deer.* Blackman, Walter, *Head of a Peasant Woman.* Boggs, Frank Myers, *Place de la Bastille* (1882). *Boats entering Dieppe Habor.* Boit, Edward Darley, *In Summer Time. Study in Normandy.* Bridgeman, F.A., *Colza Plantation in Normandy. Dune in Roumania.* Bromley, *Banks of the Thames.* Brown, W. F., *A Court at Venice.* Camp, Joseph de, *Venetian Study.* Celarie, T. F, Gaston, *Portrait of an Old Lady.* Chadwick, F. B., *Evening.* Chase, William W., *Portrait of Peter Cooper.* Coffin, W. A., *Portrait.* Conant, Cornelia W., *In the Garden.* Correja, Henry, *Asleep.* Cox, Kenyon, *Portrait. The Mirror* (portrait). Cullin, Isaac James, *Portrait.* Curtis, R. W., *Flirtation.* Dana, W. P. W., *The Beach at Etretat* (night effect). *Dutch Boat* (moonlight). Dannat, William, *After the Mass:* Davis, Charles H., *The Plain.* Deschamps, Camille, *A Little Chilly.* Desvarreux, J. L., *Normandy Pasture.* Dillon, H. P., *A Studio Seance.* Dodson, Sarah N. Ball, *The Invocation of Moses.* Dolph, John, *The Antichamber.* Donoho, Gaines R., *La Garenne. La Marcellerie.* Dubois, C. E. *Cape Martin* (near Mentone). *Red Rocks* (Mentone). Elias, Emily Wylde, *In the New Forest.* Flagg, Montague, *Portrait.* Florence, Lucien, *Head.* Gardner, Elisabeth J., *Daphnis and Chloe.* Gay, Walter, *Le Rémouleur. A Philosopher.* Gilman, B. F., *September in Calvados.* Grayson, C. P., *Going to Market.* Harrison, Alexander, *Castles in Spain. Funeral of a Redskin.* Harrison, Birge, *November. Return from the First Communion.* Heaton, A. G., *A Traveller.* Herpin, Marguerite, *Portrait.* Hilliard, W. H., *Marsh in the Landes.* Hinckley, Robert, *Alexander at Persepolis. "A la Santé du Patron."* Klumpke, Anna, *An Eccentric.* Knight, Daniel Ridgway, *Mourning.* Lancey, Ward de, *A Discussion.* Lotz, Matilda, *Dog's Head.* May, Edward Harrison, *Portrait of the Count of Uxbridge.* Melchers, J. G., *The Letter.* Mosler, Henry, *Les Accordailles* Moss, Charles E., *At Grandmother's.* Nicholls, Burr H., *Sunlight Effect. Old House at Pont-Aven* (Finistère). Ogden, Wood, *Normandy Pasture.* Pearce, Charles S., *Arab Goldsmith. Rosina.* Peirce, H. Winthrop, *Forest in February.* Pennie, Robert M., *Portrait.* Pennington, R. G., *Portrait.* Penfold, Frank, *Death of the First Born.* Reinhart, A. G., *Hut in Picardy.* Rosenthal, Toby Edward, *The Vacant Chair.* Sargent, John S., *Gipsey Dance. Portrait.* Simmons, Edward, *Study at Concarneau.* Simons, *Hunting Rendézvous.* Stewart, Jules L., *Portrait. Summer.* Strain, Daniel, *Portrait. Wild Flowers.* Weeks, Edwin Lord, *A Soudan Caravan bound for Morocco. A*

Soudan Caravan. Whistler, Neill, *Portrait.* Williams, Frederick D., *Hights of Sainte-Marguerite.* Williams, L. L., *Three Thieves.* Sketches, etc.—Boit, E. D., *Studies in Spain* (water color). Boker, Orleana Von Weissenfels. *La Sulamite* (after Cabanel). Brooks, A. F., *The Favorites* (aquarelle). Dana, Anna G., *Aged Fishermen.* Sculpture.—Bartlett, P. Wayland, *Portrait of a Lady* (bust in plaster). Ezekiel, Moses, *Portrait of Franz Liszt* (bust in bronze). Gregory, Eliot, *Portrait of a Gentleman* (bust in plaster).

1883.—Anderson, A. A., *A Widow.* Bacon, Henry, *Le Pleinariste. In Normandy.* Baird, W. B., *The Marne at Charenton. The Route to Frejus.* Baker, Ellen K., *Knitting.* Blackwith, J. C., *Cordelia.* Blackman, Walter, *Un Jour Gras.* Boggs, F. M., *Place Saint Germain des Prés. Port of Isigny.* Boit, E. D., *Bay of St. Servan at Low Tide. Cannes.* Bridgman, F. A., *La Cigale* (Fontaine's Fable). Brown, W. F., *The Gravedigger's Daughter.* Brounell, Franklin, *The Lacemaker.* Chambers, G. W., *The Shepherdess.* Chase, W. M., *Portrait of Miss Wheeler. Young Girl Reading.* Curtis, R. W., *Return from the Country.* Dannat, William, *Aragon Smugglers.* Davis, C. H., *Outskirts of the Village.* Desvarreux, J. L., *At Champbeugle.* Dodson, Sarah Paxton Ball, *Les Bacides.* Donoho, R., *Mauvaises Herbes. Primavere.* Edwards, G. W., *The Fisher's Return.* Gardner, Elisabeth J., *The Captive.* Gay, Walter, *Conspiracy under Louis XVI. The Armorer.* Grayson, C. P., *Awful Weather* (Pont Aven). Gross, P. A., *Banks of the Marne.* Harrison, Alexander, *The Amateurs. The Slave.* Herpin, Marguerite Masseras, *Game* (decorative panel). *Autumn* (decorative panel). Hinckley, Robert, *Wounded Honor. Adieu Forever.* Hoeber, Arthur, *On the Main Route.* Howe, W. H., *Normandy Cow.* King, Emma C., *Study.* Klumpke, Anna, *In the Sixteenth Century.* Knight, D. R., *Dowerless.* Lotz, Matilda, *Dogs.* Mason, L. G., *The Viaticum.* May, E. H., *Portrait of Madame Marcilly. Milton Dictating to his Daughters.* Melchers, J. G., *A Woman of Atina. Pater Noster.* Merritt, Anna Lea, *Portrait of J. R. Lowell.* Middleton, Stanley, *A Mascotte.* Monlis, Robert, *Environs of Fleury.* Mosler, Henry, *Morning of the Wedding. The Spinner.* Moss, C. E., *The Morning Prayer.* Munn, G. F., *In Brittany.* Pearce, C. S., *Prelude. Water Carrier.* Peirce, H. W., *October,* Peixotto, G. D., *Maduro. Portrait of a Gentleman.* Penfold, Frank, *The First Step. Autumn.* Pennie, R. M., *The Weaver.* Rich, J. R., *Grandmama.* Sargent, J. S., *Portraits of Children.* Shonburn, J. L., *The Shearer. Stable Interior.* Simmons, E. E., *Corner of the Market. The Winnowers.* Stewart, J. L., *Portrait of a Lady. A Court* (Cairo). Strong, Elisabeth, *Study of a Dog.* Tuke, H. S., *An Idle Day. Portrait.* Vonnoh, R., *Portrait.* Whistler, J. M., *Portrait of the Artist's Mother.* Wight, Moses, *Portrait of a Lady.* Wolff, Otto, *Ophelia.* Sketches, etc.—Curtis, R. W., *Venetian Study. Narrow Street in Venice.* Faller, Emily, *Portrait in Miniature.* Thompson, Mary, *Portrait of a Young Lady.* Wait, Florence, *Portrait of a Young Lady on Porcelaine.* Waldo, Isabel V., *Portrait of a Young Lady in Miniature.* Sculpture.—Bartlett, P. W., *Horned Crocodile of Cochin China* (bronze). Elwell, F. E., *Bust in Plaster. Rain in Spring* (bas-relief in bronze). Gates, Adeline, *Portrait* (bust in plaster). Hill, Helen, *Bust of a Lady* (portrait).

1884.—Bacon, Henry, *Let Him who Loves me Follow! He will Return.* Baird, William, *Winter in the South.* Batchelor, Nina G., *Naval Combat.* Bishing, H., *Holland Landscape.* Blackman, Walter, *Head of a Peasant Woman. Night.* Boggs, F. M., *The Old Canal at Dordrecht. On the Thames.* Boit, Edward Darley, *Grove Farm Leatherhead* (England). Bridgman, Frederick A. A., *The Family Bath* (Cairo). *Cairo Merchant.* Brown, Walter Francis, *Fisherwomen of Isigny.* Célarié, Gaston T. F., *Birds.* Chambers, George W.,

The Dunes. Cheritree, Olive E., *The Coming Storm* (Normandy). Clinedienst, B. W., *Portrait.* Coolidge, John T., *Portrait.* Copeland, A. B., *The Studio Corner.* Cranford, Kenneth R., *The Hour of Labor, Portrait.* Curtis, R. W. *Une Faintante Vénitienne.* Dannat, William P. W., *End of the Storm.* Dannat, William T., *Un Quatuor.* Deschamps, *Still Life.* Desvarreux, J. Larpenteur, *Corner of a Meadow* (Yonne). Dodson, Sarah P. B., *Portrait,* Donoho, Gaines R., *Around the Farm* (Etaples). *Ramène Ici.* Durgin, Lyle, *Portrait.* Gardner, Elisabeth Jane, *La Coupe Improvisée.* Gay, Walter, *The Apprentice. Cabbages.* Grayson, Clifford, *Ohé, le Canot!* Gross, Peter Alfred, *La Mare Renard.* Grover, Dennett, *Portraits.* Harrison, Alexander, *Twilight. The Shipwrecked of Glenans.* Herkomer, H. G., *Ready to Pose.* Herpin, Marguerite M., *Decorative Panel.* Hilliard, W. H., *Windmill* (Holland). Hinckley, Robert, *Portrait.* Howe, W. H., *Environs of Dieppe.* King, Emma C., *Portrait.* Klumpke, Anna, *Still Life.* Loving, Francis William, *Portrait.* Lotz, Matilda, *The Painter's Friends.* May, Edward H., *Will he come? Portrait.* Mills, Harry, *Farm in Normandy.* Monks, Robert H., *The Old Willows of Potigny.* Mosler, Henry, *The Last Sacrement. The Village Clock.* Pearce, C. S., *The Prayer.* Penfold, Frank, *The Widow. The First Pantaloons.* Picknell, William M., *Coast of Annisquam. Coast of Issirich.* Pilatte, Charles, *Holland Landscape in November. Near Bruges.* Poor, H. R., *Ulysses Feigning Insanity.* Reinhart, C. S., *The Mussel Gatherer. Beach at Villerville.* Sargent, John, S., *Portrait.* Simmons, *End of the Court. Spring* (decorative panel). Simmons, Vesta Schallenberg, *Corner of a Field.* Stewart, Julius L., *A Five o'Clock Tea.* Strong, Elisabeth, *The Family Dinner.* Tilton, Paul Rollin, *Seabeach in Sunlight.* Ulrich, C. F., *The Glass-Blowers.* Vail, E. L., *Fishing Harbor* (Concarneau). Weeks, Edwin Lord, *A Hindoo Sanctuary* (Bombay). *Souvenir of Jeypore.* Whistler, James, *Portrait of Miss Alexander. Portrait of Carlyle.* Wight, Moses, *An Old Document.* Williams, Frederick D., *End of an October Day.* Williams, L. L., *Why don't you eat?* Wolff, Otto, Wood, Ogden, *Le Pré Maillet* (Somme). **Sketches, etc.**—Boit, E. D., *Afternoon at Monte Carlo.* Edward, G. W., *Study of Boats.* Foote, E. K., *Ponte San Severo* (aquarelle). Williams, Frederick D., *Near the Seashore* (aquarelle). **Sculpture.**—Fry, J. H., *Portrait of a Lady* (bust).

1885.—Bacon, Henry, *Taking the Pilot.* Baird, William, *Going to Rest. Winter* (Bois de Clamart). Baker, Ellen K., *The First Effort.* Boggs, F. M., *Honfleur Harbor.* Bridgman, F. A., *Summer on the Bosphorus.* Burgess, *During the Mass* (Normandy). Butler, E. R., *Portrait.* Chadwick, F. B., *Portrait.* Chambers, G. W., *Close of Day.* Chapman, C. D., *Revery.* Coolidge, J. T., *In the Church.* Curtis, Ralph, *Interior of St. Mark's* (Venice). *In a Gondola.* Dana, W. P. W., *Heavy Weather. Calm* (night effect). Dannat, W. T., *Portrait of a Lady.* Davis, C. H., *Evening Quiet.* Derrick, W. R., *Marine Study.* Dillon, H. P., *Portrait of Madame Harry Alis.* Dixwell, Anna Parker, *Still Life.* Dubois, C. E., *Foot of Mount Pelegrino* (Palermo). *Ruins of a Greek Theater* (Sicily). Espey, Edward, *Rest.* Field, E. L., *In Brittany.* Fry, John, *Samson.* Gardner, Elisabeth J., *Corner of the Farm.* Gay, Walter, *The Spinners. November.* Gregory, Eliot, *Portrait of Mrs. Sherwood.* Grayson, C. P., *Fisher's Children.* Hale, Ellen Day, *An American Winter.* Harrison, Alexander, *The Seashore. A Wave.* Healy, G. P. A., *Portraits.* Herkomer, H. G., *Portrait.* Hoebert, Arthur, *"Daily Bread."* Howe, W. H., *Morning in September.* Hubbard, Mary Whitwell, *Portrait.* Klumpke, Anna, *Portrait.* Knight, D. R., *The Babblers.* Lancey, Ward de, *Mother Antoine.* Lasar, Charles, *Canal near Coutances.* Lotz, Matilda, *The First Breakfast.* May, E. H., *The Penitent Thief. Pandora.* Melders, J. Gari,

The Toilers of the Sea. Meza, Wilson de, *Portrait of a Lady. A Street in Brittany.* Mills, Harry, *Portrait.* Mosler, Henry, *The Coming Storm.* Niles, E. G., *Portrait of a Lady.* Parker, S. H., *Father John* (Normandy). Pearce, C. S., *Heartache.* Peixotto; G. D. M., *Portrait of Cardinal Manning.* Platt, C. A., *Studio of an Aquafortist.* Reinhart, C. S., *On Sunday.* Rosenberg, H. M., *Consolation.* Rosenthal, T. E., *Departure of the Family* Donoho, Ruger, *In the Clover.* Rudell, P. E., *Autumn.* Sargent, J. S., *Portrait of a Lady. Portrait of two Girls.* Shonborn, Lewis, *Prison Gate* (Tunis). Simmons, E. E., *Low Tide.* Simmons, Vesta Schallenberg, *Breton Children.* Singer, Winaretta, *The Gravel Lands* (Villerville). Stewart, J. L., *A Hunting Ball.* Story, Julian, *Odalisque.* Strong, Elisabeth, *Waiting for the Master.* Theriat, C. J., *Portrait.* Tolman, Stacy, *A Normandy Garden.* Uhl, S. J. *Cour de la Reine* (Rouen). *View of Dieppe.* Vail, E. L., *The Outer Harbor* (Dieppe). Ward, William de Lancey, *La Mère Antoine.* Watrous, H. W., *The Summing Up.* Weeks, E. L., *The Last Voyage* (reminiscence of the Ganges). Whistler, James, *Portrait of Lady Archibald Campbell. Portrait of Theodore Duret.* Williams, *Morning Visits.* Wood, Ogden, *A Picardy Pasture.* **Sketches, etc.**—Boit, E. D., *Rain Storm in the Rue Royale.* Dana, C. E., *Farm near Etretat* (aquarelle). *Breton Fishing-boat* (aquarelle). McEwen, Walter, *Danseuse.* MacKnight, W. D., *Five Landscapes* (aquarelle). **Sculpture.**—Boyle, John J., *Portrait* (bust in bronze). Elwell, F. E., *Water Carrier of Pompeii* (statue in plaster). Gales, Adeline, *St. John* (plaster statuette). Hall, C. Winslow, *Youth* (bust in plaster). Taft, Lorado, *Ste. Genevieve in Infancy* (statue in plaster). *Portrait of a Clergyman* (bust in plaster).

1886.—Albright, Adeline, *Portrait de Madame H.* Bacher, Orro H., *Palazzo Cadora* (Venice). Bacon, Henry, *Jack Ashore.* Baird, William, *In the Forest. The Head of the Family.* Baker, Ellen K., *The Mussel-Gatherer. Infancy.* Barnesley, J. M., *Entering Dieppe Harbor.* Batchelor, Nina G., *Alas, poor Yorick!* Besnard, Paul F., *Pond in the Loiret* (morning effect). Bishing, Henry, *The Banks of the Zuyderzee. A Dutch Meadow.* Blashfield, Edwin Howland, *Autumn* (decorative panel). Boggs, F. M., *Fishing Boat. Windsor Castle.* Boit, E. D., *Monte Carlo.* Boott, Elisabeth, *Still Life. Portrait.* Brewster, Amanda, *Morning in Autumn.* Bridgman, F. A., *The Embroiderer* (Moorish interior). Butler, H. R., *Evening in October. Gathering Seaweed* (evening effect). Chadwick, F. B., *Morning in October.* Curtis, R. W., *Sirocco at Venice.* Dana, William P. W., *Naval Combat* (episode of the War of 1812). Danforth, Charles, *Les Bavardages. Allez-donc, Mollie.* Dannat, William T., *Portrait of Madame Dannat. A Sacristy in Aragon.* Davis, C. H., *Evening. The Last Reflections.* Denman, Herbert, *The Trio.* Dillon, H. P., *Cabaret du Chat Noir.* Donoho, Ruger, *Portrait of the Author.* Durgin, Lyle, *Portrait of Miss D.* Fairchild, Mary Louise, *Portrait of Miss S. H.* Fox, Charles Lee, *A Prayer.* Gardner, Elisabeth J., *The Imprudent.* Gay, Walter, *The Weaver. My Last Price.* Gregory, Eliot, *Portraits of the Children of Mrs. J.* Gross, P. A., *The Seine at Carrières Saint-Denis.* Hamilton, J., *Portrait.* Harrison, Alexander, *In Arcadia.* Harrison, Birge, *The Hallali.* Harrison, E. Ritchie, *Mère Honoré.* Healy, G. P. A., *Portrait of the Honorable McLane, United States Minister to France. Portrait of the Consul General of the United States.* Howe, William H., *A Normandy Bull. Cows* (Normandy). Klumpke, *Portrait of a Young Lady.* Knight, Daniel Ridgway. Lotz, Matilda, *Hunting Dogs.* McEwen, Walter, *Returning from Labor. The Judgment of Paris.* Major, Ernest L., *A Landscape.* May, Edward H., *Portrait of Madame H.* Melchers, Julius Gari, *The Sermon.*

Middleton, Stanley, *Portrait*. Mills, Henry, *Young English Fisherman*. Newman, Carl, *Portrait*. Noreross, Eleanor, *Portrait*. Parker, Stephen Hills, *Two Portraits*. Parrish, Stephen, *On the Rance* (Brittany). Patrick, J. D., *Study*. Pearce, C. S., *Shepherdess* (Picardy). Phelps, Helen W., *The Cloister*. Rhodes, *Return of the Carrier Pigeons*. Santry, D. F., *The Weelwright*. Sargent, John S., *Portraits*. Sawyer, Roswell Douglas, *Still Life. Souvenir de Pennedepie* (Calvados). Simmons, E. E., *Number Three. A Breakfast* (Spain). Simmons, V. S., *The Bird Catchers*. Singer, Winnaretta, *Portrait*. Smith, De Coste, *Sioux Vedettes watching a Wagon Train*. Smith, John Lewis, *Gathering Seaweed* (storm effect). Stark; Otto, *Who goes There?* Stewart, J. L., *Full Speed*. Strickland, Charles Hobart, *Portrait*. Strong, Elisabeth, *On the Track*. Theriat, C.J., *Portrait*. Truesdell, Gaylord S., *The Chair-Mender*. Vail, E.L., *On the Thames*. Edwin Lord, *Imperial Cortege returning from the Grand Mosque of Delhi*. Wentworth, Cecilia E., *Portrait of General McClellan. Portrait of a Lady*. Whiteman, J. Edwin, *Winter*. Whistler, *Portrait*. Whitwell, Mary Hubbard, *Portrait*. Wigand, Otto Charles, *The Mushroom Gatherer* (Brittany). Williams, L. L., *An Offering*. Wood, Ogden, *The Hour of Repose*.
Sketches, Cartoons, etc.—Dana, Charles E., *Lynmouth, England* (water-color). *Banks of the Lynn* (water-color). Field, *The Water's Edge*. Greatorex, Kathleen, *The Russian*. Knight, D. R., *Peasant Girl. Three Studies in Water-Color*. Lasar, *Study*. Parker, Stephen Hills, *Graziella* .(pastel). Pearce, C. S., *A Road at Auvers-sur-Oise* (pastel). **Sculpture.**—Bartlett, Paul W.; *Two Portraits of Ladies* (plaster). Bissell, *Statue* (bronze). Boyle, John J., *The Age of Stone in North America* (group in plaster). Donoghue, John, *Young Sophocles Leading the Choir of Victory after the Battle of Salamis* (plaster). Mezzara, Joseph, *Bust of a Lady* (marble).

1887.—Allen, Thomas, *On Guard*. Anderson, A. A., *Portrait of General Howard*. Bacon, Henry, *At the Capstan*. Barnsley, J. A., *Afternoon at Butteaux* (Oise). Beckwith, J. C., *Portrait of Mr. Walton*. Bisbing, Henry, *At the Barrier*. Blake, Mabel, *The Chimney Corner*. Blackmann, Walter, *Head of a Young Woman*. Boggs, F. M., *The Thames near Greenwich*. Brewster, Amanda, *A Village Incident*. Bridgman, F. A., *On the Terrace*. Butler, H. R., *Moonrise. The Sea*. Chadwick, F. B., *Five O'clock*. Cheritree, Olive E., *In Normandy*. Clark, T. S., *Le Fou du Fou*. Clarkson, R. E., *Villagers Receiving the News*. Curtis, R. W., *Evening at Venice*. Dana, W. P. W., *The Namouna*. Damforth, Charles, *A War History*. Dannat, W. T., *Portrait of M. Laplante*. Davis, C. H., *The Last Rays*. Smith, de Cost, *Amorous Sioux*. Dillon, H. P., *Foundation of the Order of the Jesuits*. Dodson, S. P. B., *The Morning Stars*. Donoho, Ruger, *Sous Bois*. Dow, A. W., *A Field in Finistère*. Fairchild, Mary, *Confidences*. Gardner, Elisabeth J., *The Farmer's Daughter. Innocence*. Gay, Walter, *Presenting a Petition to Richelieu. A Master Stroke*. Goodman, A. J., *Ophelia*. Gross, P. A., *Pond of Vaux de Cernay*. Halle, H. W., *A Canal at Venice*. Harding, D. B., *Portrait of Mademoiselle Nathalie. Study*. Harrison, Alexander, *Twilight*. Harrison, E. R., *Portrait of an Australian Lady. Une Matelotte d'Etaples*. Hassam, Childe, *A Shower*. Healy, G. P. A., *Portrait of the Austrian Ambassador, Count Hoyos. Portrait of M. Barbedienne*. Howe, W. H., *Return of the Cows at Evening*. Kavanagh, John, *A Shepherd. A Woman of Scheveningue*. King, Emma, C., *Study*. Klumpke, Anna, *Catinou in the Black Mountain* (Tarn). *Stable Interior*. Knight, D. R., *October*. Loomis, Eurilda, *Preoccupied*. Loring, F. G., *Little Shepherd*. MacEwen, Walter, *Dutch Courtship. The Trompette of Amsterdam*. Marcy, W. L., *Portrait of a Young Lady. Portrait of a Lady,*

Mathews, Arthur F., *Imogen and Arviragus. Portrait of a Gentleman.*
May, E. H., *Portrait of a Gentleman.* Melchers, J. G., *In Holland.*
Middleton, Stanley, *"School's In !" Portrait of a Young Lady.* Monks,
Robert, *The Marsh.* Mosler, Henry, *L'Abandon: Visit of the Marquise.*
Munsell, A. H., *Bad Weather.* Newman, B. T., *Lunch in Brittany.* Page,
W. G., *Meditation.* Parker, S. H., *Portrait of Mademoiselle Gabrielle Logé.
Portrait of a Young Lady.* Pearce, C. S., *Ste. Geneviève.* Reid, R. L., *The
First Communion.* Reinhart, C. S., *A Wreck. A Seabird.* Robinson,
Theodore, *Daily Bread.* Sawyer, R. D., *Turf-pits of the Somme. Autumn
in Picardy.* Scott, E. M., *Still Life.* Sewell, R. V. V., *Winter.* Simmons,
E. E., *Age and Infancy.* Simmons, F. W., *Head of a Young Girl.*
Simmons, Vesta, *Landscape.* Singer, Winnaretta, E., *On a Balcony. Portrait.*
Slade, Emily, *Portrait of a Young Lady. My Concierge.* Small, F. O.,
Death of the First Born. Smith, A. P., *The Well-known Road.* Stark,
Otto, *Evening.* Stewart, Edward, *Fields of Veules-en-Caux.* Stewart, J. L.,
Study. La Berge at Bougival. Stokes, F. W., *Study of a French Interior.*
Stone, William, *Sunset at Gretz. By the Bridge* (Gretz). Strong, Elisabeth,
The Comrades. Portrait of a Cat. Tojetti, Virgilio, *In the Coulisses.*
Truesdell, G. S., *Cows at Pasture.* Vail, E. L., *Widow.* Weeks, E. L.,
Bayaderes (Bombay). Wenzell, A. B., *The Orphan Girl.* Whiteman, S. E.,
Winter Morning on the Banks of the Essonne. Wigand, Otto C., *Réflexion
après le Pardon.* Williams, Elisabeth, *Portrait of the Artist's Mother.* Wood,
Ogden, *Marsh in Seine-Inférieure.* Wright, Frederick, *In Brittany.*
Sketches, etc.—Dana, Charles, E, *Two Aquarelles.* Munsell, A. H.,
Portrait of Madame H. Stewart, J. L., *Portrait of a Young Lady* (pastel).
Sculpture.—Adams, S. H., *Portrait* (bust in plaster). Donoghue, John,
Nymph of the Chase (statue in plaster).

ADDENDA. (1884).—Dellenbaugh, F. S., *Fishing Encampment at Sea. Play-
ing Truant.* (1887).—Foster, Ben., *Forest of Fontainebleau.* Hitchcock,
George, *The Tulip Culture.* Patrick, J. D., *Jerry.* Shonborn, Lewis, *Playing
Truant.* Strickland, C. H., *Portrait of a Gentleman.*

List of American Artists Honorably Rewarded at the Salon and Living in 1886.

Medals.—Bierstadt, Albert; Bridgman, F. A., (3), (2); Church, F. E., (2);
Dana, W. P. W.; Danna', William; Gardner, Elisabeth J.; Healy, G. P. A.
(3), (2); May, Edward S.; Pearce, Charles Sprague; Sargent, John S. (2);
Whistler, James McNiel.

Honorable Mentions.—Butler, H. R.; Chase, William; Dennian,
Herbert; Gardner, Elisabeth J.; Gay, Walter; Greatorex, Kathleen; Harrison,
Alexander; Howe, W. H.; Klumpke, Anna; McEwen, Walter; Mosler, Henry
(*at the Luxembourg*); Picknell, W. L.; Simmons, E. E.; Smith, L. J.; Stewart,
Julius L.

Honorable Mentions, 1887.—Beckwith: J. Carroll; Chadwick,
Francis, B.; Davis, Charles H.; Hitchcock, George; Reinhart, Charles S.

Bierstadt, Bridgman, Church, Healy, and Sargent are *Hors Concours.*

Guerlain's Perfumery is at 15 rue de la Paix.

CHURCH AND CHARITABLE WORK.

The Americans in Paris have been among the foremost in every benevolent work. They have given freely of their money and their time, and when occasion required have not spared personal effort. They have contributed as individuals, as Churches, and as relief societies. The ladies of the Colony have co-operated in the sympathetic and self-denying manner characteristic of the gentler sex. The Church of the Holy Trinity has its Dorcas Society. The American Church in the rue de Berri has its Sewing Circle. The Missionary Association of the latter has received and distributed 135,325 francs. An American lady has taken personal charge of a branch of the Young Men's Christian Association in the rue Jean-Jacques-Rousseau intended to supply the moral needs of young women. The Anglo-American branch of this association, is at 160 rue Montmartre. It numbers among its officers three Americans, Professor Yeatman, Rev. W. W. Newell and L. C. McAfee of San Francisco. Rev. Drs. Morgan and Hough are on the Advisory Board. Americans at home and abroad contribute generously to its maintenance. The Churches in the United States carry on their mission labors in Paris through the agency of the McAll Mission, the pioneer impulse having been given by Miss Elisabeth R. Beach a young American lady who had previously been a member of the Colony. Rev. Dr. Beard formerly pastor of the American Church gave to it largely of his effort and influence. Mr. and Mrs. Newell, Mrs. Le Gay and other members of the American Churches in Paris have actively co-operated. The Rev. Dr. Hough is a member of the Board of

Directors. The mission held 3,886 services in 1886 with an aggregate attendance of 497,383. Several *Salles* are supported by the American cities whose names they bear, the Salle Philadelphia at No. 23 Rue Royale, the Salle New York at No. 10 Boulevard Sébastopol, the Salle Baltimore at No. 8 Boulevard Bonne Nouvelle, and the Salle Washington at No. 62 Rue Monge. There is also the Salle Beach at .59 Avenue Wagram named after the young lady whose influence has been so potent in the origin and successful propagation of the mission work. Sketches of the American churches and relief societies follow.

THE AMERICAN CHURCH.

The American Chapel was founded in 1857 to supply the want of an undenominational place of worship for Americans living in Paris. A suitable edifice was erected in the Rue de Berri whose doors were opened in an entirely undenominational spirit to all those who desired to unite in Christian worship, fellowship and work. Ten years later it was organized on the basis of the International Evangelical Alliance, its creed being the statement of doctrine adopted at the first conference in London in 1846. The Episcopalians who formed part of the original congregation finding the service not sufficiently ritualistic separated themselves and built in the Rue Bayard and afterwards in the ave de l'Alma. Since the Church was recognized in 1868, 798 persons have been added to its membership in various ways. It has received representatives from nearly all the dissenting denominations of Great Britain and from all the Protestant denominations of America realizing in this manner the idea of the American alliance. It observes the Christian ordinances by maintaining public worship, preaching religious doctrine, giving moral instruction to the young, visiting the sick and ministering to the wants of the poor regardless of creed and nationality. It has engaged generously in mission and charitable work. In 1881 the edifice was renovated at a cost of seventy thousand francs or about its original cost. It is now called the American Church in Paris. Services are held every Sunday at 11 a.m. The Church has had the following pastors since 1857 :—Rev. Dr. E. N. Kirk, Jan. 1857 to Sep. 1857 ; Rev. Dr. R. H. Seeley, Jan. 1858 to

Oct. 1859; Rev. Dr. G. L. Prentiss, Dec. 1859 to June 1860; Rev. Dr. John MacClintock, assisted by Rev. Andrew Longacre, June 1860 to April 1864; Rev. Dr. Byron Sunderland, June 1864 to Oct. 1865; Rev. Dr. Burlingham, Nov. 1865 to May 1866; Rev. Dr. Azariah Eldridge, June 1866 to April 1868; Rev. Dr. C. S. Robinson, May 1868 to July 1871; Rev. Dr. E. W. Hitchcock, March 1872 to Jan. 1883; Rev. Dr. A. F. Beard, March 1883 to Dec. 1885; Rev. Dr. J. W. Hough, Dec. 1885, still the pastor.

CHURCH OF THE HOLY TRINITY.

The Americans living in Paris before the Empire worshiped in a church in the Rue d'Aguesseau built in 1847 by Bishop Luscomb of the English communion. The Bishop transferred this property to the Rev. Mr. Chaumier also of the Established Church in. consideration of a life-annuity. He died six months later and Mr. Chaumier came into full possession. The revenues of the proprietor and pastor accrued from an admission fee of one franc paid by every person attending divine service for which tickets were duly issued at the door after the manner of a theater. In 1853 Mr. Chaumier fearing fatal results from a surgical operation to which he found it necessary to submit, proposed to Dr. Thomas W. Evans that the Americans, who were an important element of the congregation, should purchase the church. Accordingly, Dr. Evans furnished the necessary security, and preliminary arrangements were made, pending the execution of documents necessary to perfect the title. The price agreed upon was $45,000. Before legal measures were completed for the transfer, some English residents of Paris to whom the church had previously been offered by the pastor and peremptorily refused decided that an effort should be made to retain it in the English communion. Dr. Evans consented to forego his claim, and the money needed for the purchase was raised by Englishmen, Lord Cowley, then British Minister to France, and Queen Victoria contributing generously. But the idea of an American church was not abandoned. A committee was at once formed of which Rev. Dr. Kirk was chairman. A site was purchased in the Rue de Berri on which the American chapel was erected, and as the congregation was to be composed of various Protestant denominations it was agreed that the service should be ritualistic though not in exact conformity with the canons of the Episcopal Church. Some years afterwards the Episcopalians, who were a large and wealthy element, thought best to separate themselves and have a place of worship of their own. This led to the erection of the church in the Rue Bayard which was dedicated in 1866. It was a small but elegant building costing $30,000 and having a seating capacity of two-hundred and fifty. It is interesting to remember in this connection that the Emperor and Empress, who were always kind to Americans, expressed personal interest in both these buildings, and smoothed away every obstacle that the authorities might have raised to their erection. In both cases it was expressly stipulated that they should be exclusively devoted to public worship according to the ritual of the Protestant Episcopal Church. The building in the rue Bayard satisfied the religious wants of the Colony for nearly twenty years. In 1882 the project of a larger and handsomer building whose cost was not to exceed $150,000 began to be discussed. A site was purchased in the avenue de l'Alma, and the work commenced. The modest plans of the original projectors were not adhered to. Personal ambitions and the desire for a "pillared fane" or grand temple to the Deity led to radical changes in the vestry and finally to the construction of the present massive pile of masonry at a cost of more than half a million dollars. The expense was considerably increased by grave errors in regard to material so that the building cannot now be said to represent the money expended on it. It was dedicated in November 1886. It is of sufficient size the seating capacity being over one thousand. The style of architecture is old English Gothic. It is to be regretted that the exterior is less attractive than the interior since by its external aspect it will be chiefly judged by foreigners who will regard it as an exponent of American taste in art and architecture. The auditorium is elegantly finished and not without a certain beauty inherent in the style though greater lightness of detail might possibly have comported better with the sunnier doctrines of modern theology. The service which, when the society was first organized, was moderate in form has undergone some notable modifications and has now become severely ritualistic. A pleasant feature of it is the music which is rendered by a choir of boys carefully drilled. The Sunday audiences comprise many of the best representatives of the Colony in Paris with a large number of travelling Americans inclined to devotion. A considerable part of the money needed to complete the church came from persons living in America some of whom own pews or in other ways contribute to the support of the pastor and the various expenses necessary to the carrying on of public worship. The persons financially responsible for the land were Dr. Thomas W. Evans, Colonel Ritchie and Dr. Morgan The contracts for the building were secured by the signatures of Levi P. Morton, Dr. Thomas W. Evans, Henry White and Dr. Morgan. The church has never had but two pastors, Rev. Mr. Lamson and Rev. Dr. John B. Morgan.

THE CHARITABLE FUND ASSOCIATION.

The Charitable Fund Association was organized in 1869 with the object, as stated in the constitution, of "raising and maintaining a fund by subscription or otherwise for the purpose of aiding and relieving such unfortunate and indigent citizens of the United States of America as may be found in the city of Paris requiring and deserving such aid and assistance." Its first reunion, on mention of Rev. Mr. Lamson, was held on the twenty-second of February following in order to associate the society with a national holiday dear to all Americans. Persons paying twenty francs were declared entitled to membership. Those contributing one hundred francs became life members. The by-laws provided as follows for the expenditure of the relief funds: Application was to be made to a member of the Executive Committee, who being satisfied himself that the claim was legitimate was to send it at once to the Secretary who was authorized if the case were urgent to call a meeting of the Executive Committee within twenty-four hours.

The original executive comprised the following officers: President, Dr. Thomas W. Evans; Vice-Presidents, George T. Richards and James Phalen; Treasurer, H. A. Shackelford; Secretary, William Schwartz; Executive Committee, William O. Lamson, Charles S. Robinson, John Harjes, Charles B. Norton, Edward R. Andrews, Nathan Appleton, W. E. Johnson, Alfred Lockwood, Henry Woods. The following are the names of the original members:—

Thomas W. Evans.	John A. Dix.
James McKaye.	Anson Burlingame.

William O. Lamson.
W. Pembroke Fetridge.
Charles Pepper,
Alfred Lockwood.
Charles S. Robinson.
Theodore S. Evans.
Ferdinand Lawrence.
H. O. Brewer.
Charles Toppan.
A. C. Downing.
John Savage.
William Schwartz.
Edward Dart.
John W. Crane.
James W. Tucker.
G. J. Bucknall.
Edward R. Andrews.
William de Groot.
Parke Godwin.
J. C. Kane.
John Munroe.
C. A. Du Bouchet.
George T. Richards.
J. Q. A. Warren.
James Phaler.
H. A. Shackelford.
Philip H. Coolidge.
Wickham Hoffmann.
Charles B. Norton.
J. W. Dix.

John A. Dix.
John A. Harjes.
Eugene Winthrop.
R. B. Lowry.
E. W. Andrews.
George Kemp.
William Heine.
John Stearns.
W. Wurts Dundas.
W. E. Johnson.
Wright E. Post.
George H. Howard.
Robert S. Meeks.
Henry Woods.
Nathan Appleton.
John Garcia.
Charles S. P. Bowles.
Frank Livermore.
Edward A. Crane.
Wed. W. Clarke.
H. J. Griswold.
L. C. Austin.
J. Kremer.
C. D. Smith.
M. Laugel.
Maurice Strakosch,
George W. Childs.
Marion H. Cumming.
Horace J. Fairchild.
M. Chadwick.

A report of the Secretary published in 1885 shows that there were seventy-nine persons relieved during the fiscal year ending April fourth, 1876, one-hundred and twenty during the twelve months that followed, one-hundred during the succeeding seven months, and three-hundred and thirty-six persons or families during the two years beginning November fourth, 1877. A large part of these were furnished with means to return to the United States or to go to other countries. Nearly the same numbers were assisted in different ways during the corresponding periods that followed till 1885 when it was found that, besides many hundreds who had received pecuniary aid in miscellaneous ways, two-hundred and thirty-eight persons had been sent to their homes in the United States, and two-hundred and thirty-nine to England or other countries where they would be able to support themselves. The Executive Committee at the date in question included Dr. Thomas W. Evans, President; Colonel James McKaye, Vice-President; Louis Von Hoffman, Second Vice-President; William Seligman, Robert E. Turner, G. P. A. Healy, C. E. Detmold, Theodore W. Evans; Henry S. Spencer, Treasurer; Edward A. Crane, Secretary.

THE RELIEF SOCIETY OF THE UNITED STATES.

The Relief Society of the United States of America was organized by some American gentlemen to whom it seemed desirable that the United States Minister to France should be the official head of a charitable association intended to aid Americans in distress. Its rooms are at 235 rue du Faubourg St. Honoré. From an official report made in 1885 it appears that one hundred and ten persons had been assisted during the previous year either with money or with means to return home or to go to different parts of Europe where they hoped to be able to support themselves. The officers at this date were: Honorary President, Hon. Robert McLane, United States Minister; Honorary Vice-President, Hon. George Walker; Treasurer, John Munroe; Secretary, J. L. R. White. Executive Committe: F. A. Bridgman, W. Coleman Burns, R. W. Corbin, E. A. Dodge, G. H. Draper, C. A. Goodwin, Benj. Hart, William Herrick, H. S. Homans, W. A. Hopkins, J. W. Hough, D.D., John C. Kane, Edmond Kelly, John W. Mackay, J. B. Morgan, D.D., G. P. Munroe, John Munroe, James Phalen, Wright E. Post, Harrison Ritchie, M. A. Sorchan, H. A. Spaulding, F. A. Starring, Theodore B. Starr, William H. Stewart, George St. Amant, J. W. A. Strickland, J. L. R. White, J. H. White.

THE TRAVELLERS' CLUB.

The Travellers' Club was formed in 1886 for the purpose of affording a place of meeting for those who adopted the constitution. Nothing could have been simpler. The number of members was limited to two hundred. Permanent members pay on entering a sum of five hundred francs, three hundred as a subscription to the club, and two hundred as entrance fee. The management is entrusted to a committee of twelve members elected at a general meeting. The president is chosen for one year and can be re-elected indefinitely. Meetings for political objects and political discussions are not allowed. One great source of discord is by this means excluded. Baccarat and similar games of chance are forbidden, a rule that is strictly adhered to. Ambassadors and foreign ministers accredited to the French Government may be admitted as members on their application, by a resolution of the committee simply, and as permanent or temporary members according to their choice. The Club-rooms are opened at eleven a.m. No one is admitted after one in the morning. The Club furnishes breakfast and dinner to which any member can invite his friends. Elaborate banquets to distinguished personages are not given. The object of the members is quiet and retirement which they have secured by establishing a series of sensible rules and insisting on their observance. The Travellers' Club is the only one in Paris that can be considered exclusively American, other clubs originally American having gradually lost that character and those in which Americans still form an important element are so cosmopolite as to have the special features of no particular nation. The Club occupies commodious rooms at 32 Avenue de l'Opera.

BOARD OF DIRECTION.

President, Lorillard Spencer; *Vice-President*, Benjamin Hart; *Treasurer*, J. C. Kane; *Secretary*, Edmond Kelly; *Committee*, H. I. Barbey, I. Brasseur, Geo. H. Draper, De Courcy Forbes, Benjamin Hart, W. S. Kernochan, J. C. Kane, Edmond Kelly, George Morgan, Lorillard Spencer, J. R. D. Shepard, Clarence Warden.

MEMBERS.

H. I. Barbey, I. Brasseur, G. Binder, A. Belmont, Capt. A. de Bourbel, H. Cachard, S. W. Cragg, John Lee Carroll, Geo. H. Draper, Thos. E. Davis, P. de la Chaise, V. de Lungo, J. C. Dodge, E. G. Field, De Courcy Forbes, F. Gebhard, Paul Grahame, Ogden Goelet, H. S. Homans, Benjamin Hart, F. A. Havemeyer, John Iselin, Augustus Jay, W. S. Kernochan, J. C. Kane, Edmond Kelly, Lorillard Spencer, J. R. D. Shepard, Alfred Slidell, T. B. Starr, Suarez Santos, A. R. Twombley, J. F. Loubat, L. L Lorillard, F. Lawrence, George Morgan, W. Marston, John Munroe, F. Munroe, George P. Munroe, C. Meletta, Capt. Piffard, C. R. Penniman, C. K. Pettis, S. W. Pomeroy, Harrison Ritchie, J. C. Runkle, Gen. Meredith Read, Clarence Warden, Eugene Winthrop, J. le Roy White, Bronson Willett, Eliot Zborowski.

MINISTERS AND SECRETARIES OF LEGATION.

The following list includes the names of all Ministers and Secretaries of Legation who have represented the United States at Paris since the acknowledgment of the Republic by foreign Powers.

Thomas Jefferson Minister Plenipotentiary left Paris for America September 26, 1789 having served about two years. The duties of the office were performed by William Short, Secretary of Legation, till the accession of Gouverneur Morris in January 1792.

Morris was succeeded by James Monroe who assumed the duties of the office May 28, 1794. Monroe was recalled Aug. 22, 1796 and took his leave the following December.

Charles C. Pinckney of South Carolina arrived in December 1796 but the Directory refused to receive him. John Marshall of Va. and Ellbridge Gerry of Mass. were associated as Commissioners and authorized to treat with the Directory but failed on account of the chicanery of Talleyrand. Pinckney and Marshall returned to America in April 1798. Gerry followed in July.

Oliver Ellsworth of Conn., William Vans Murray of Md. and William R. Davis of S. C. were appointed Joint Envoys and Ministers to the Consulate in 1799. They left Paris in October, 1800. James A. Bayard, of Del. was appointed but did not serve.

From Oct. 2, 1801, to Nov. 18, 1804, the office of Minister was filled by Robert R. Livingston. He was succeeded by John Armstrong of N. Y. who remained till Sept. 4, 1810. After his departure Jonathan Russell Secretary of Legation was Chargé d'Affaires till Joel Barlow came as Minister in Feb., 1811. Barlow died at Zarnovics Dec. 28, 1812. William C. Crawford came as Minister in April 9, 1813, and took leave April 22, 1815. Henry Jackson of Kentucky, Secretary of Legation was in charge of the

Legation till the accession of Albert Gallatin July 9, 1816, who filled the office of Minister for years. Daniel Sheldon of Conn. being Secretary of Legation.

During the reign of Charles X., James Brown of Louisiana was Minister and John A. Smith of Mass. Secretary of Legation.

During the reign of Louis Philippe which continued 18 years the American Ministers were William C. Rives of Va., Edward Livingston of La., Lewis Cass of O., and William R. King of Ala. The Secretaries of Legation were C. C. Harper of Md., Nathaniel Niles of Vt., and Leavitt Harris of Pa. under the first; T. P. Barton of Pa. under the second; C. P. Anderson of N. Y. and Henry Ledyard of Mich. under General Cass, and J. L. Martin of N. C. under Mr. King.

Richard Rush of Pa. was Minister to the Republic of 1848. He left Paris in 1849, and was succeeded by William C. Rives of Virginia who took leave in 1853. Stephen K. Stanton served as Secretary of Legation with Mr. Rush.

The Ministers under the last Empire were as follows, taking office at the dates stated : William C. Rives of Va., July 20, 1849 (left 1853) ; John Y. Mason, Oct. 10, 1853 ; Charles J. Faulkner of Va., June 16, 1860; William L. Dayton of N. J., March 18, 1861 ; John Bigelow, March 15, 1865 (having been chargé d'affaires from Dec. 21, 1864); John A. Dix, Sept. 24, 1866 ; Elihu B. Washburne, March 17, 1867. The two ministers succeeding Mr. Washburne were Edward F. Noyse who came in 1872 and Levi P. Morton who came in 1881.

The Secretaries of Legation during the period were Henry S. Sanford of Conn., Donn Piatt, of O., O. Jennings Wise of Va., J. B. Wilbor of N. Y., W. R. Calhoun of S. C., James G. Clarke of N. H., Robert M. Walsh of Pa., William L. Dayton jr. of N. J., William S. Pennington of N. J., George P. Pomeroy of N. Y., Wickham Hoffman of La., John W. Dix jr. of N. Y. and Frank Moore.

The Government of the United States is (1887) represented in Paris by Robert McLane of Maryland, Minister Plenipotentiary; Henry Vignaud, First Secretary of Legation ; Augustus Jay, Second Secretary of Legation ; George Walker, Consul General, Robert M. Hooper. Vice Consul. Mr. Walker was succeeded July 1, 1887, by J. L. Rathbone of California.

RULES FOR SOCIAL GUIDANCE.

The following brief treatise on good manners has been derived from various sources, French, English and American. It is sufficiently complete and comprehensive to satisfy the ordinary demand for information of the character. The rules by which polite society is governed have a general resemblance among the people of all nations the basis on which they rest being necessarily the same everywhere. There are differences of detail usually of minor importance. There is much to commend in the French code of politeness and the manner in which it is observed. The respect for parents and superiors which it inculcates is beyond praise. It is something to be noted by American youth with whom frankness of spirit and independence of manner sometimes degenerate into impoliteness. No less worthy of imitation are the forbearance, the gentleness of manner, and the courtesy evinced by the French in their relations to one another. Though Americans may not deem it advisable to obey all the rules and regulations enumerated by French writers on etiquette, it must be admitted that these have now or have recently had, their *raison d'être*. They are the result of centuries of social attrition and scrupulous ceremonial observance, and therefore merit respect. In some cases differences have been indicated ; in others French writers have been followed without remark. It is needless to say that Americans living in Paris and mingling with its society need to understand its ceremonial code their personal associations often rendering its partial or complete use obligatory.

Of Good Manners.—Good manners were originally the mere expression of submission from the weaker to the stronger. In a rude state of society every salutation is to this day an act of worship. Hence the commonest acts, phrases, and signs of courtesy with which we are now familiar, date from those earlier stages, of our life as a nation when the strong hand ruled, and the inferior demonstrated his allegiance by studied servility. Let us take for example the words "Sir" and "Madam." "Sir," once in use among equals, but now only proper on the lips of inferiors, is derived from Seigneur, Sieur, Sire, and originally meant Lord, King, Ruler, and, in its patriarchal sense, Father. The title of Sire was last borne by some of the ancient feudal families of France who, as Selden has said, "affected rather to be styled by the name of Sire than Baron, as Le Sire de Montmorenci and the like." Madam, or Madame, corrupted by our servants into "Ma'am," and by Mrs. Gamp and her tribe into "Mum," is in substance equivalent to "Your exalted," or "Your Highness"—*Ma Dame* originally meaning high-born or stately, and being applied only to ladies of the highest rank.

We take off our hats on meeting an acquaintance. We bow on being introduced to strangers. We rise when visitors enter our drawing-room. We wave our hand to our friend as he passes the window, or drives away from our door. The Oriental, in like manner, leaves his shoes on the threshold when he pays a visit. The natives of the Tonga Islands kiss the soles of a chieftain's feet. The Siberian peasant grovels in the dust before a Russian noble. Each of these acts has a primary, an historical significance. The very word "salutation," in the first place, derived as it is from *salutatio*, the daily homage paid by a Roman client to his patron, suggests in itself a history of manners. To bare the head was originally an act of submission to gods and rulers. A bow is a modified prostration. A lady's courtesy is a modified genuflection. Rising and standing are acts of homage, and when we wave our hand to the friend on the opposite side of the street, we are unconciously imitating the Romans who as Selden tells us used to stand "somewhat off before the Images of their Gods solemnly moving the right hand to the lips and casting it, as if they had cast kisses."

Men remove the glove when they shake hands with a lady, a custom evidently of feudal origin. The knight removed his iron gauntlet, the pressure of which would have been all to harsh for the palm of a fair *châtelaine*, and the custom which began in necessity has travelled down to us as a point of etiquette.

How are we to define that unmistakable something, as subtle as an essence, that makes a gentleman or a gentlewoman? May good breeding be acquired as an art? and if so, where are we to seek the best professors? Who does not wish to give his children, above all other accomplishments that inestimable branch of education, the Manners of Good Society? What is learning, what are abilities, what are personal attractions, what is wealth, without this one supreme essential? A man may know as many languages as Mezzofanti, may have made scientific discoveries greater than those of Herschel or Darwin, may be as rich as a Rothschild, as brave as a Napier, yet if he has a habit of hesitating over his words, or twisting his limbs, of twiddling his thumbs, of laughing boisterously, of doing or saying awkward trifles, of what account is he in society? So likewise of a woman. Though she were fair as Helen, skilled in all modern accomplishments, well-dressed, good-natured, generous, yet if her voice were over-loud, or her manner too confident; above all, if she were to put her knife in her mouth at dinner, who would think of her beauty, or her accomplishments, or her fine clothes? Who would invite her? Who would tolerate her?

Neither gestures, nor tones, nor habits, can be accepted as infallible signs of good or ill breeding. Thumb-twiddling, and lolling, and knife-swallowing, are terrible habits enough, and would be, of course, sufficient to exclude any man or woman who practised them from the precincts of good society; not only because they are in themselves offensive, but because they would point to foregone associations of a vulgar kind; but they do not of necessity prove that the primary essentials of good manners, the foundation, so to speak, upon which the edifice of good manners should be built, is wanting in those unfortunate persons who are guilty of the offenses in question. That foundation, that primary essential, is goodness, innate goodness, innate gentleness, innate unselfishness. Upon these qualities, and these alone, are based all those observances and customs which we class together under the head of Good Manners. And these goods manners, be- it remembered, do not merely consist in the art of bowing grace- fully, of entering a room well, of talking easily, of being *au courant* with all the minor habits of the best society. A man may have all this, know all this, and yet, if he be selfish, or ill-natured, or untruthful, fail altogether of being a true gentleman. Good manners are far, indeed, from being the outward evidences of mere training and discipline. They are, *au fond*, the kindly fruits of a refined nature. As just and elevated thoughts expressed in choice language are the index of a highly trained and well- regulated mind, so does every act, however unimportant, and every gesture, however insignificant, reveal the kindly, considerate, modest, loyal nature of the true gentleman and the true lady. Hear what Ruskin has to say of the characteristics of the true gentleman : "A gentleman's first characteristic is that fineness of structure in the body which renders it capable of the most delicate sensation, *and of that structure in the mind which renders it capable of the most delicate sympathies*—one may say, simply, 'fineness of nature.' This is, of course, compatible with heroic bodily strength and mental firmness; in fact, heroic strength is not conceivable without such delicacy. Elephantine strength may drive its way through a forest, and feel no touch of the boughs; but the white skin of Homer's Atrides would have felt a bent rose-leaf, yet subdue its feelings in glow of battle, and behave itself like iron. I do not mean to call an elephant a vulgar animal, but if you think about him carefully, you will find that his non-vulgarity consists in such gentleness as is possible to elephantine nature; not in his insensitive hide, nor in his clumsy foot, but in the way he will lift his foot if a child lies in his way; and in his sensitive trunk, and still more sensitive mind, and capability of pique on points of honor. . . . . Hence it will follow, that one of the probable signs of high breeding in men generally will be their kindness and mercifulness; these always indicating more or less firmness of make in the mind."

Introductions.—Ladies of social equality are presented to each other, and so also are gentlemen. When the difference between the parties is doubtful, the person introducing may say : " Mrs. F. this is Mrs. X.; Mrs. X., Mrs. F.," thus striking a balance of respect.

A gentleman desiring to be introduced to a lady, must first obtain permission, after which the following formula may be used : " Mr. Arthur desires to be presented to Miss Angell." If the lady making the introduction desires the mutual acquaintance of the parties, she says : " This is Mr. Harmon, Mrs. Enfield. It gives me pleasure to present him to you." The married lady replies according to her feeling, and, of course, in terms of polite conversation. If she is pleased to know Mr. Harmon, she says so cordially and frankly, at the same time thanking the presentee, who withdraws at once.

A young lady in the same circumstances politely recognizes the gentleman, bows and smiles, using the name of the new acquaintance. The gentleman alone can express gratification, adding such compliments as the occasion seems to demand. The introduced parties may be as friendly as they please, but excessive cordiality on first acquaintance is not to be commended.

The etiquette of hand-shaking is simple. A man has no right to take a lady's hand till it is offered. He has even less right to pinch or retain it. Two ladies shake hands gently and softly. A young lady gives her hand, but does not shake a gentleman's, unless she is his friend. A lady should always rise to give her hand ; a gentleman, of course, never dares to do so seated. On introduction in a room, a married lady generally offers her hand, a young lady not.

In a ball-room, where the introduction is to dancing, not to friendship, you never shake hands, and as a general rule, an introduction is not followed by shaking hands, only by a bow.

It may perhaps be laid down that the more public the place of introduction, the less hand-shaking takes place ; but if the introduction be particular, if it be accompanied by personal recommendation, such as, "I want you to know my friend Jones," or, if Jones comes with a letter of presentation, then you give Jones your hand, and warmly too. Lastly, it is the privilege of a superior to offer or withhold his or her hand, so that an inferior should never put his forward first.

If the difference in age between two ladies or two gentlemen be unmistakable, the younger is presented to the elder. If there is an admitted superiority, the disparity in age is unobserved. The unknown person is presented to the man of greater fame without question.

The single lady is introduced to the married lady, and the single gentleman to the married, other things being equal.

Persons born and reared in the best society never make a hasty presentation or introduction. An habitual though momentary reflection adjusts in their own minds the proper relation of the two who are about to be made known to each other, and unpleasant mistakes thus become almost impossible.

Introductions should be considered wholly unnecessary to a pleasant conversation. Every person should feel that he is, at least for the time, upon a social equality with every guest who is present. That a person was bidden to the entertainment proves that the host so considers him, and the acceptance of the invitation levels him, for the time, either up or down to the social grade of all who he may meet, no matter at what estimate he may hold himself when elsewhere. A lady or gentleman must conduct himself or herself, while remaining in the house, as if there was no more exalted society than that which is present.

Salutations. "A bow," says La Fontaine, "is a note drawn at sight. You are bound to acknowledge it immediately, and to the full amount." According to circumstances, it should be respectful, cordial, civil, or familiar. An inclination of the head is often sufficient between gentlemen, or a gesture of the hand, or the mere touching of the hat ; but in bowing to a lady the hat must be lifted. If you know people slightly, you recognize them slightly ; if you know them well, you bow with more cordiality. The body is not bent at all in bowing, as in the days of the old school forms of politeness ; the inclination of the head is all that is necessary.

There are many things in connection with the French habits of saluting that are gentle and graceful. Persons lift their hats upon coming into a place public or private where there are others who must be at once conscious of their presence and nearness. They bow when they take their places near others in public parks or gardens. They salute unobtrusively when entering or leaving cafés, restaurants, or dining-rooms that are not crowded and where their movements are necessarily noticed. It is considered, if not imperative, certainly in excellent taste to lift the hat slightly when passing others in narrow walks, passages or on staircases where there is likely to be the slightest contact or jostling. This is in some sense an apology for unintentional trouble or annoyance and the salutation should be quiet, modest, and entirely without effort at formal politeness.

One's own judgment ought to be sufficient as to the *empressement* of the salutation. In bowing to a lady, the hat is only lifted from the head, not held out at arm's length for a view of the interior. If smoking, the gentleman manages to withdraw his cigar before lifting his hat ; or, should he happen to have his hand in his pocket, he removes it.

Gentlemen who are driving are obliged to keep a tight hold of the reins, and this is impossible if they remove their hats. A well-bred foreigner would never dream of saluting a lady by raising his whip to his hat. American gentlemen have adopted this custom, but it would be still better if they would set the fashion of bowing without touching the hat or raising the hand, when holding the reins.

A well-bred person bows the moment he recognizes an acquaintance. According to the rules of good society everywhere, every one who has been introduced to you is entitled to this mark of respect. A bow does not entail a calling acquaintance; to neglect it shows neglect of early education.

In thoroughfares where persons are constantly passing, gentlemen keep to the left of a lady, without regard to the wall, in order to protect her from the jostling elbows of the unmannerly; unless a lady prefers to walk on the gentleman's left, *for his protection*.

A gentleman walking with a lady returns a bow made to her (lifting his hat not too far from his head), although the one bowing is an entire stranger to him.

It is civility to return a bow, even if you do not know the one who is bowing to you.

Should any one wish to avoid a bowing acquaintance with a person who has once been properly introduced, he may do so by looking aside, or dropping the eyes as the person approaches, for if the eyes meet there is no alternative.

Bowing once on a public promenade is all that civility requires. At the second meeting, if you catch the eye of your acquaintance, smile slightly. If the gentleman is an acquaintance it is better to avert the eyes.

A lady may permit a gentleman who is walking with her to carry any very small parcel that she has, but never more than one.

A lady cannot take the arms of two gentlemen, nor should two ladies take each one arm of a gentleman, " sandwiching " him, as it were.

Gentlemen do not smoke when driving or walking with ladies, nor on promenades much frequented.

A married lady should always extend her hand to a stranger brought to her house by a common friend, as an evidence of her cordial welcome. Where an introduction is for dancing there is no shaking of hands.

A gentleman when stopped by a lady does not allow her to stand while talking with him, but offers to turn and walk with her.

When a gentleman joins a lady on the street, turning to walk with her, he is not obliged to escort her home. He can take his leave without making any apology.

Never give the cut direct unless for some inexcusable rudeness. It is better to meet a recognition coldly.

A lady may recognize a gentleman who has been formally presented to her, even when he cannot recall her face, on account of the difference of appearance made by the change from gaslight to daylight. His acknowledgment of her recognition must be as respectful as to a valued friend.

The same formalities obtain at entertainments. The gentleman, who is a formal acquaintance, waits patiently for the lady guest to recognize his presence.

Cards and Invitations.—Letters informing a person of a birth, marriage or death, if the recipient is not sufficiently intimate to render a visit in person, should be replied to within a week by card. If the letter conveying the information is from a person at a distance it should be replied to by a note of congratulation or of condolence. If the letter does not include an invitation to the church only a card in reply is necessary. An invitation to dinner requires a response only in case of refusal. If accepted, only a card is necessary. An invitation to a ball or party requires a formal reply whether the person invited accepts or not. The person who has attended a ball or concert should, say the French authorities on social matters, send his card within a week if he does not desire to return, or make a formal call if he wishes to retain the acquaintance. The French code requires that a card be sent to a person who has just been advanced in official position, or has suffered a stroke of misfortune. A noble act generally remarked should receive similar recognition. Visiting cards should be as simple as possible. Some authorities say that those of men should always have their address; those of women, never. On these points there is a difference of opinion. Cards bordered with black should invariably be used when the person is in mourning. Cards can with propriety only be sent by post at the beginning of the new year. At that epoch the sending can continue till the fifteenth of January. At Paris the turning of the upper right corner implies a visit, the partial folding of it, as in England, a call upon the family. When a person is ill cards should be left at the door and his health asked for. When going to the country one leaves cards for his friends marked *P. P. C.* Returning cards are left for all those a retention of whose acquaintance is desired. When persons are presented in society and are requested to visit those to whom they are presented cards should be left on the following day if it is intended to accept the invitation. When it is desired to recognize a courtesy they should be left in person, or sent by a servant, the corners not being turned. In what is here said only two modes of manipulating cards are recognized, the folding, and the turning of the upper right corner. In New York the card manual is more intricate. There turning the upper right corner implies a visit, that is a call in person; the upper left corner, congratulations; the lower right corner, adieu; the lower left corner, condolence; the entire right end, a call on the family. No more than three cards should be left at the same time on members of the same family. Visiting cards should always be engraved, printed on the finest material, and not too small. It is in better taste to omit the prefix *Mr.*

Of Visits in General.—Parisian writers on good breeding suggest that a visit of ceremony should not exceed fifteen minutes in length. If it is made to a person in position and he is occupied one should leave immediately without giving the slightest sign of annoyance. Visits near the dinner hour should not be prolonged. Calls on parents who have given invitations to the nuptials of their children should be made within two weeks. A month is allowed to return an ordinary visit. New-Year's visits to grandparents and superiors are paid in France on the thirty-first of December. Visits to the hostess who has given a dinner should be made within a week. If indisposition prevents the exercise of this courtesy excuses should be made in writing. Calls should not be made on those having a calling-day at any other time unless in case of intimate friendship. An invitation to a party should be recognized by a call within a month if it is desired to maintain the acquaintance. The hour for calling varies according to circumstances. At Paris it is from three to six ; in the provinces from two to five. Gentlemen call in the evening except at those houses where there is, a day for receiving. In Paris these visits are made in full dress. If made in the daytime nothing should be worn that belongs exclusively to the evening. When making a call and others are in the drawing-room, there should be no private conversation among those seated side by side. It would be a discourtesy to the hostess. The conversation should be general. The visitor should withdraw during a lull in the conversation attracting as little attention as possible. Guests already seated should not rise at the entrance of others, the hostess alone doing the honors of the salon. The hostess should never resign her chair except to some one whom she holds in profound respect. If on the occasion of a call she is busily occupied with intimate friends, it should be made as brief as possible unless others arrive in the meantime.

Miscellaneous Rules for Visits.—Self should never except in case of absolute necessity be the subject of conversation. A person should never seem to be seeking compliments. Arrived in the country calls should be made on those who have come before if it is wished that social relations be maintained. Calls from those who arrive later should be awaited. This is the rule generally in Europe. In America the custom is reversed on the theory that the newly arrived are comparative strangers and the laws of hospitality demand they should be so greeted. This rule has the merit of corresponding with Oriental observances almost as old as the world. Gentlemen coming to make a call leave their outer garments in the vestibule and enter the salon, the hat in the hand. A lady leaves in the vestibule her umbrella and over-shoes if it has been found necessary to wear them. If persons are present the visitor bows slightly on entering the salon, then advances to salute the hostess, waiting if offered a seat, till she herself is seated. A gentleman keeps his hat in his hand during the entire visit. He need not wait till a seat is offered. He can take a chair of his own accord being careful that it be not too near that of the hostess. He should never seat himself beside her unless expressly asked. A gentleman should rise when a lady enters. A lady never rises, but bows slightly. European etiquette requires that when a visit is made to an important personage every one should rise when he or any member of his family, even the youngest, enters the reception-room. In parting the hostess never accompanies her visitor beyond. the door of the salon, even if it be a prince. Such courtesy is only paid to extreme age or high ecclesiastical position. In France New Years' calls are made on the first of January only to the members of one's family including aunts and elder-sisters. A week is allowed to call on cousins or other relations by blood or marriage; a fortnight to call on friends, the entire month to visit mere acquaintances. These visits should not, it is said last more than five or ten minutes. It is not thought to be in good taste to wish a Happy New Year unless the call is made on the first of January.

Presentations and Visiting Deportment.—The person presenting another to the hostess should approach her, bow, and say "Permit me to present to you Mr. and Mrs. X. who greatly desire to · make your acquaintance." If it is a gentleman who makes the presentation French etiquette requires that he use the words "I have the honor to present, etc." If there are titles they should be used instead of the words Mr. and Mrs. The French language in this matter is more absolute and artificial. The English is more flexible, and, if the idea is preserved, permits variations from the form, the person making the presentation being presumed to be perfectly at his ease and in no danger of uttering phrases *mal-a-propos*. The person presented bows respectfully, and if it is a lady, salutes gracefully and replies amiably to the kind reception accorded by the host and hostess. A lady thus presented awaits the visit of the lady whose acquaintance she has thus made. An invitation to a dinner or a ball renders a visit unnecessary. A visitor finding himself with others at the door of a salon should not insist on his right of precedence. The eldest ladies go first. Young ladies give place to widows and to those who are married. The men come last in the order of their age. Gloves should not be taken off before making a call. The ornaments and objects of art in a salon should not be too curiously regarded. A person recovering from an illness owes a call on all those who have left their cards in the meantime. Visitors in Paris making a call in their own carriage send a valet to ask of the concierge if the person sought is in. If the carriage is hired they make this inquiry in person. Calls of condolence are expected of all those who have been informed by letter of the death of friends or acquaintances, unless the recipient is in full mourning. Children should never accompany those making visits of condolence. Ladies making them should wear dark colors, gentlemen dark gloves. In France if the call is made on a gentleman, the gentlemen embrace the gentlemen, and the ladies extend the hand. If upon a lady, the ladies embrace, and the men shake hands. The health of the person called upon is not asked after, and the dead is only spoken of after the person in mourning has introduced the subject. The conversation should be quiet and reserved corresponding as far as possible with the situation. A person not being able to make a visit of condolence on account of being in deep mourning sends a letter of sympathy by a messenger. Intimate friends may call upon the bereaved on the day of burial. Two weeks should elapse before calls are made by others. Visits of condolence should be extremely brief.

Morning Receptions.—The custom of having a particular day for receiving is now the rule though contrary to abstract theories of politeness. A hostess should not under any plea be absent on the day selected and announced. The reception should be in the salon and the house in perfect order. In case of illness the most intimate friends should not be received lest the action should be misunderstood. The hostess receives in modest toilet in order not to outshine her guests.. An artist may have a special day for receiving in his studio owing to the necessities of his occupation. The custom of announcing the names of visitors in a loud voice at the door of the salon has been abandoned in Paris. Instead the host or hostess presents them to one another. When a lady enters, the hostess rises and indicates a seat, waiting till the guest is seated before she sits again herself. If the host is present he conducts the lady to her place. The hostess bows without rising when a gentleman enters and with a slight gesture indicates a chair unless it be an old man or a distinguished person when she follows the form required for her lady visitors. If several enter at the same time attention is first paid to those whose age or position in the world demand the highest consideration. The lady of the house takes the place at the right of the hearth yielding it to no one unless to a grand personage or to an older relation. The places of honor are near her. The place at the left of the hearth is only given to an aged lady. The host can yield his place to a lady, never to a gentleman. When a lady withdraws the hostess rises and accompanies the departing guest into the corridor or anti-chamber. If alone she goes only to the door of the salon. If other guests are present she only rises, salutes, and does not reseat herself till the visitor has passed the threshold. The hostess never asks a gentleman to lay aside his hat. She never talks aside with any of her guests, and endeavors to lead the conversation of those present away from disputed questions of politics and religion, or matter that might wound the feelings of any one. She parts with her guests with a gentle reluctance. When they rise to leave she rings promptly for the servant to conduct them to the door.

Of Dinner-Giving. — Invitations to a dinner should be sent eight days in advance. They are sent in writing only to equals and inferiors. To those to whom special respect is due they are given at a visit made in person. If a guest is unable to accept, the vacancy can only be filled by an intimate friend unless a week still remains before the day appointed. When the dinner is served the mistress of the house offers her hand to the most dintinguished or eldest guest. The host offers his arm in the same manner to the lady to whom he owes the greatest respect on account of her rank or age. The master of the house goes first, the mistress always last. In returning to the salon the mistress precedes. Places at table are indicated by cards. When all are at their chairs they remain standing till the mistress gives the sign to be seated. Host and hostess are always *vis-à-vis*. If the hostess is a widow she places opposite her, her father, her uncle, an aged relative or a friend of long standing, and never a young man unless it is her son. A widower places in front of him, his mother, an aged female relative or a friend advanced in years. The oldest or most notable guests should have the places at the right of the host and hostess, usually those persons with whom they have entered the dining-room. Other places should be assigned as nearly as possible in accordance with age or rank. The tact of the hostess is displayed in complying with these conditions and in placing guests according to their own preferences and sympathies. All guests are equal in the eyes of the entertainer. Dishes should be served without praise or excuse. Invitations to partake should be cordial but not too persistent. The dinner should be the best that the fortune of the host permits. Strict etiquette asks nothing more. The mistress of the house serves the dessert. Conversation should be based on the principles established for morning visits, the situation owing to the grouping about a common table being even more delicate and often requiring the exercise of the greatest tact on the part of entertainers.

General Observations.—Breakfasts and suppers are less formal, unless given on the occasion of a wedding or some other ceremonial. Invitations are less discriminate. Tea, coffee, or chocolate should invariably be served. Wines are not exacted at a breakfast *en règle* in France but the best possible at a supper. At a supper less attention is paid to a regular succession of dishes. Soups and salads are not ordinarily served, and dishes in France are usually cold. In England and America more latitude is allowed. It is hardly necessary to say that considering the hour, everything offered to the guests should be light and digestible. Invitations to break-fast if the number of guests is limited ought to be given in person during the previous week, and only such a number should be asked as can be entertained without crowding. Thirteen persons only should never be invited or placed at table, not out of respect to the superstition but from consideration for the possible preju-dices of some of the guests. A formal dinner should always be served by male servants in full dress. Livery should never be worn on such occasions. Servants should never be spoken to by the master or mistress during a repast, and under no circum-stances reproved no matter how maladroit. An invitation to a friend to dinner should include that friend's relatives living with them or their guests. If this is not possible at the moment they should be included in a later invitation. Only at French dinners of the most intimate character is it permitted to the host to retain his male guests at table after the ladies have retired to the drawing-room. Even if he does this he should first offer his arm to the lady at his right to conduct her to the salon, after which he returns to his friends in the dining-room. A good host and hostess will always bear in mind the remark of Brillat-Savarin: " To invite one to dinner is to make yourself responsible for his happiness for the entire time that he is under your roof."

Rules for Guests at Dinner.—Persons invited to dinner should arrive at the hour appointed. It is bad breeding to arrive before, or to keep others waiting by coming too late. A gentleman should never offer his arm to the lady of the house when dinner is announced. She invariably chooses her cavalier. A lady should never refuse the arm of a gentleman who offers it to accept that of another. It would be a grave insult. The lady going to table with the host should never pause to allow another to pass before her. If an aged lady has failed to find her proper place in descending to dinner it belongs to the lady before her, and not to that lady's cavalier to see that a pause is made that she may pass. If places have not been indicated by cards the guests before approaching the table should wait till they are pointed out by the hostess. Then all arrange themselves behind their chairs and await the signal to be seated which the hostess gives by seating herself. Gentlemen wait until all the ladies are seated. The lady unfolds her napkin before the gentleman beside her. The napkin is never entirely unfolded and remains upon the knees. A reasonable distance from the table should be maintained. Care should be taken not to jostle those near you. The elbows should be kept close to the sides. Ladies should keep their skirts within bounds. An erect attitude should be maintained, and a certain degree of self-control always manifest. The wines served should simply stimulate or inspire the conversation and not be allowed to cause a moment of self-forgetfulness. Bread should be broken over the plate, never cut. A plate already served sent by the mistress to a guest should not be passed to another. The quality of the food should not be commented on. If not to the taste it should be left on the plate. French authorities are not entirely agreed on the manipulation of the fork though most agree that it should be retained in the left hand the right being necessary for cutting the food and, to change it from left to right requires an ungraceful movement. The knife should never be used for lifting the food to the mouth. A gentleman should always attend to the wants of the lady at his side, but unobtrusively. A lady should never seem too solicitous that those about her be served, that being the duty of the domestics. If the assistance of a servant is needed, wait till he looks in your direction and make your wants known by a sign. Servants should not be thanked when they offer the dishes, since they occupy only an intermediate position between the guest and the host. As little noise as possible should be made in eating, and nothing whatever should be done that may draw special attention. One ought not to say in offering a dish to a lady "Mrs." or "Miss do you want this?" but, "Allow me to offer this to you." The first formula is reserved for servants. The knife and fork should be left on the plate after each course if it is the custom of the house to change them so often ; if not they should be left on the knife-holder.

Points of Taste and Breeding.—When talking at table avoid gestures or speaking in a loud tone. Allusions to other and better repasts are in bad taste. A story intended for all the guests should only be related at the invitation of the host or hostess. A too serious and personal conversation should not be carried on by a young gentleman with a young lady at his side. Preference should never be expressed for any part of a joint of meat or of a fowl unless it is intimated by the host nor should a dish be asked a second time. No effort should be made to cool a dish that is too warm. If a dish is offered for a guest to serve himself he should do so modestly, and with the knife and fork that are with it. A gentleman should not ask a lady to partake of his fruit. A lady can take this liberty with a lady of her acquaintance. At a restaurant it is sometimes permissible to test the wine by its odor, never at a gentleman's table unless he calls your attention to its bouquet. Toasts at private tables can only be proposed by the host. If it is in champagne wine at dessert the glass is raised and the guest regards the hostess before touching it to his lip. If the host proposes a toast everyone raises his glass and bows slightly. If the toast is addressed to a lady she only bows slightly. If the toast is to the master or mistress of the house all the guests bow slightly toward them, the men drain their glasses, the ladies merely touch them to their lips. Guests rise from table only when the hostess has given the signal. The napkin is left beside the plate. The gentlemen offer the left arm to the ladies. If a lady has already accepted that of the gentleman at her left she inclines her head without speaking. All return to the salon in the order in which they left it. Guests should not leave the house after the end of the dinner for at least two hours. French etiquette in this respect differs in unimportant details from the rules followed in England and America. Calls in France can be made within the two weeks following the dinner, which should be returned within a month by persons of fortune, widows without means, young ladies and bachelors only being exempt from the exercise of this courtesy.

Parties and Balls.—Invitations to a large party should be sent fifteen days in advance. It is not deemed in good taste in France to invite a priest to a ball or other reunion where ladies are to be *décolletées.* Persons invited inform the lady who has done them the honor whether they accept or decline. If they are present they send their cards once more within a week after the party. It is not desirable to arrive too early at a party. Ladies who are obliged to attend several the same evening should spend but a short time at each, ending with the most important. Their toilet should be arranged according to the houses they visit. Young women are not expected to go to *soirées* or balls unless accompanied by their husbands, mothers, or some lady advanced in years. It is the rule in France. A young lady may go with her sister if the latter is accompanied by her husband, and if a young lady is on terms of great intimacy with the persons giving the entertainment she may go alone arriving before any other guest can reasonably be expected. The hostess remains at the door of the salon to receive her guests till dancing begins. She should wait and should not dance while there are other ladies unprovided with partners. A gentleman asked by the hostess to be the partner of a lady can never refuse. It is not polite to ask a lady to dance just at the moment the music begins. A lady who has declined to dance on the plea of fatigue should not dance again during the evening. A gentleman should not pass his arm about the waist of a lady before the commencement of the waltz or polka. A lady who has by mistake accepted two invitations to dance the same number should refuse both and remain seated till it is finished. It would be unbecoming for either gentleman to seek to make her change her resolution. It would be an impertinence for a gentleman who has been refused by a lady to ask another near her who is aware of the refusal to dance unless it was because of insufficient acquaintance or he is able to pass over the *contretemps* with a pleasant jest. A young lady who does not dance should remain near her mother or chaperone.

Suggestions.—A lady should never give her bouquet, her fan, or her handkerchief to a gentleman to hold while she is dancing unless he be her husband, her brother, or a near relation. As soon as a waltz or polka ceases a gentleman should remove his arm from about the waist of the lady. When a lady wishes to be seated it is a mistake for her partner to request her to dance again. He should simply escort her to her place and express his regret in the simplest terms. A gentleman who dances badly should not invite a lady to dance with him who is unaware of the fact. A gentleman who has taken the place that a lady has left for the purpose of dancing should leave it during the closing measures that she may not be compelled to reclaim it. If the mistress of the house and her daughters dance they should be the first asked. If they decline for the time, without fixing the question of precedence, invitation should be renewed from time to time during the evening. It is an impertinence to affect to despise dancing. It is not permitted a gentleman by Paris etiquette to offer his arm to a young lady to conduct her to the buffet or across the salon. He can never offer his arm to a very young lady unless she is an acquaintance and is received at her house. Gloves should be removed at supper or at the buffet but not to partake of refreshments passed during the evening.

Concerts.—If music is to form a part of the entertainment at a party and a person is able and is asked to take part he should do so or remain at home. A person asked to accompany a singer on the piano should manifest no desire to attract attention. A person should not take his place at the piano to turn over the leaves of the music unless at the singer's request. A host or hostess should receive the artists invited to assist at a party as guests whether they are paid or not. Concert toilets are the same as those at a formal dinner or a small party. At a concert no matter how brilliant ladies wear a hat or bonnet. Young girls only can appear without head-covering. Persons arriving at a concert while a number is being rendered should wait till its close, from respect to the artists as well as the master and mistress of the house guests should be quiet during the music. It is ill-bred to beat time or

to hum the air while artists are singing. A person who has
consented to sing or play at a party should submit his selections
beforehand to the hostess for her approval. A hostess should
acknowledge her indebtedness to those who have gratuitously
assisted at her concerts by inviting them to dinner, sending them
a box at the theater or opera or some tasteful gift if the person
is in moderate circumstances, giving in such a manner that it
does not seem like the payment of an obligation.

Asking in Marriage.—The asking of a young lady's hand in
marriage is considered in France a matter of extreme delicacy, in
the management of which the young man should be careful to
avoid the slightest error. If he has met a young lady in society
whom he desires to espouse he asks a common friend to ask her
in marriage of her parents. This step can in no case be taken
by the person himself. If the friend brings back a refusal the
question remains stationary. If the young man knows no one
who is on intimate terms with the family his request may be
proferred by the priest, pastor, or rabbi according as the family is
Protestant, Catholic or Hebrew, or even to the family's notary.
No matter by whom his suit is pleaded it is indispensable that he
be recommended to the parents by some one whose testimony is
indisputable. If the reply is favorable he asks to be presented,
and this introduction takes place when the young lady is not
present. At this first visit material affairs only are treated of.
The father or guardian of the young lady questions the young
man as to his position, his fortune, his occupation, etc. These
details having been communicated the father or guardian declares
the replies satisfactory and states the amount of the young lady's
dowry and her expectations. Then they invite him to return
fixing the day for his next visit. If the parents are not satisfied
with the suitor's responses the amount of the dowry is not stated
and time is asked for reflection. The suitor cannot insist directly
or indirectly. He patiently awaits the decision and if it is in his
favor presents himself at the hour named neatly but uncere-
moniously dressed.

The Meeting.—The hour for the meeting has been so arranged that no other persons will be present. The young lady is simply but elegantly dressed. She has been made aware of the demand for her hand but no allusion is made to it at this meeting. If this interview is agreeable to the young man he asks through his family that he be admitted to the house of the young lady as her formal suitor, or *prétendu*. This request is made by the young man's father, or by his mother if she is a widow, by a near relation or even by a friend. The consent of the young lady's parents having been obtained the young man presents himself to thank them at an hour previously arranged. The young lady is not present when he arrives, but after thanks have been expressed and he has been finally accepted, she is summoned and presented to the suitor as his future wife. This presentation is a matter of form merely she having been previously informed to avoid surprise or disappointment. Thenceforward the accepted suitor is admitted to intimate though not familiar relations with the family. The distinction is delicate. He may come often but must make his visits carefully dressed while the destined bride must never meet him in *négligé*. They cannot call one another by their given names but must always add *Mr.* and *Miss* when they address one another. If for grave reasons there is a rupture in these relations the causes should be concealed with care. Some plausible pretext should be given for the cessation of the visits such as an illness or a journey. Then a letter should be written to the young lady's father or guardian expressing respectfully the great regret felt at being forced to withdraw for family reasons that do not admit of explanation. If the young man when he makes his first visit sees reasons for discontinuing his suit he writes to the family on the following morning not a letter of refusal but stating that he is going away on a brief journey. Once admitted to the house as *prétendu* he comes often, always ceremoniously, announcing himself with a bouquet which he sends to his *fiancée*. Applications for the hand of a widow or a young lady who is her own mistress should not be made to herself, but through her notary or an intimate friend. No visit should be made till a response is received. If the reply is favorable a bouquet should be sent with a note asking when a visit will be convenient. A marriage should be kept secret till the contract is entirely arranged, and only a few days before the affixing of the signatures should it be formally announced to friends. Thenceforward the young lady should not be séen in society or at the theater, and the house of her parents is closed except to the family of the affianced husband and intimate friends.

Contract and Corbeille.—The contract is usually signed at the office of the notary except in the case of families of importance when that official comes to the house of the parents of the *fiancée*. Custom is not fixed on this point. If the notary comes to the house to witness the signing of the contract he is invited to dinner. The price of the contract formerly depended on the value of the dowry. The notary now leaves it to the generosity of his clients. The bases of the contract should be previously agreed on. If there is a misunderstanding afterwards the negotiations should be discontinued politely and without any manifestations of ill-will. All expenses pertaining to the marriage acts are payable by the future husband. After the notary has read aloud the contract the future husband rises and salutes his *fiancée* as if to ask her approval, then signs and offers her the pen. After her sign in the following order the mother of the intended husband, the mother of the *fiancée*, the two fathers, and after them the members of the two families according to age. On the same day the young man sends the *corbeille de mariage*. Then there should be a fête at which the gifts, mingled with flowers, are shown to friends in the young lady's chamber. A discreet man should not make presents of extraordinary value. Formerly a sum was expended for this purpose amounting to five per cent. of the money; at present ten per cent. is so expended. The gifts comprise shawls, jewels, laces, furs, gloves, fans, and a purse containing a certain sum in new gold pieces. They are displayed in a handsome box or on a table intended to form part of the furniture. They are sent with a bouquet on the morning of the day that the contract is to be signed. If there is a *fête* on that day the *fiancée* should appear at it dressed in white. If there is a dancing party, the ball is opened by the affianced couple dancing as partners. The *fiancée* dances the second *contredanse* with the notary, a substitute for his former privilege of being the first to kiss the bride. A bridal gift is expected of all those who sign the contract.

Going to the Church.—Weddings at Catholic churches in Paris and in the large provincial cities of France take place on Tuesday, Thursday and Saturday between six in the morning and one in the afternoon. If it is desired that the wedding take place on some other day application must be made to the Curé. The church selected is usually that in the parish where the young lady resides. Time and place must be in accordance with the rules and regulations of the Romish Church. The bridegroom and his family should come to take the bride and her relatives. He offers her the wedding bouquet made entirely of white flowers. Carriages employed by him seek relatives of the two families to convey them to the residence of the bride whom they must accompany to church. The expenses attending the ceremony are at his charge. The breakfast after mass, the great family dinner, the party and ball are given by the bride's family. The bridegroom coming to seek his bride brings with him the wedding-ring which is of gold or silver according to the fortune of the couple. In small villages a sou supplies the want of a ring which is blessed by the priest during the ceremony. When all are assembled who are to be present at the wedding, the cortege departs going first to the Mairie to procure the bulletin of civil marriage afterwards given to the priest. The first carriage contains the bride who occupies the righthand corner on the back seat. Her mother is beside her. Her father occupies the front sea. If she is motherless the place is supplied by a lady of her acquaintance. In the second carriage are the bridegroom and his family, the mother occupying the righthand corner on the back seat and having her son at her left. The father or the witnesses occupy the front seat, or the witnesses occupy the third carriages and are followed by the other carriages containing relations and friends.

At the Altar.—Alighting at the church door the father of the bride, or he who replaces him gives her his arm to conduct her to the altar. The bridegroom follows with his mother, then the mother of the bride with the father of the bridegroom or with the bridegroom's first witness. The witnesses give their arms to the nearest relatives, those of the bridegroom to the lady relatives of the bride and reciprocally. In passing before their guests bride and bridegroom bow slightly without turning the head. Reaching their places in the choir the bridegroom takes his position at the right, the bride at the left, the family of each placing themselves beside them. Only relatives and most intimate friends can occupy the reserved seats in the choir. Other guests take chairs as near as convenient. The priest addresses to the bride and groom the question : "Do you agree to take," etc. Before replying each turns respectfully toward the father and mother, and respectfully salutes them, then replies in a low tone at the same time bowing slightly toward the priest. When the priest blesses the ring, bride and bridegroom remove their gloves. Then the bridegroom bending forward takes with his right hand the ring which the priest gives him, and places it on the ring-finger of the bride. Both rise and taking in their right hands the tapers before them and advancing to the altar place the money offered in the hands of the priest. After the *Pater* the canopy is held over their heads while kneeling at the *prie-dieu* by the youngest sons of the two families placed according to relationship. In going to the sacristy to sign the act of marriage and receive the congratulations of friends the procession is formed in inverse order to that on entering, that is the father of the bridegroom or his first witness escorts the bride, and the mother of the bride takes the arm of the bridegroom. In leaving the sacristy the newly married go together, then the father or first witness of the bridegroom with the bride's mother. The order for entering or leaving church is the same whether the ceremony be according to Protestant or Jewish rites.

Rules for Subsequent Conduct.—If friends present at the church have not been invited to accompany the bride home they should be conveyed to their own residences by the carriages employed for the occasion. Persons invited to a wedding at church should call and congratulate the family issuing the invitation within a week. If from being in mourning, sickness or other causes it is impossible to attend the marriage ceremony letters of excuse must be sent. Cards can only be sent if one is or wishes to remain a stranger to the family. Black should not be worn at a wedding at church unless brightened by other colors in such a manner as to show that it is not mourning. The bridegroom is expected to wear gloves, not white but *beurre frais*. Guests should arrive and be in their places when the wedding cortege enters. The deportment of every one during the ceremony should be befitting the place and occasion. It is less the custom than formerly for the newly wed to go on a journey immediately after the ceremony at church. If they go at all they wait till evening. In such case there is an informal breakfast given by the bride's mother to which the father and mother of the groom and his two witnesses are invited. At this repast bride and groom sit side by side. At the dinner, which is *de rigueur*, they are placed *vis-à-vis*. At the right of the bride sits the father of her husband or the person who fills his place, that is to say his nearest relative who has acted as his first witness, and at her left her own father. If an important personage has been invited she should have a place of honor beside the husband if it is a lady. Witnesses are placed as near as possible. The bride should be first served. One of the witnesses of the bride offers the first toast to her, and one of the witnesses of the groom performs the same office to him. The father of each replies for his child. These speeches should be prepared beforehand. Guests at a wedding-dinner invite the newly married to a dinner or *soirée* before leaving. It is called a *rendu de noce*. If a widow marries her daughter while still in mourning she must wear at the ceremony a toilet of gray and white. If a ball is given on the wedding-day it is opened by the bride with the friend whom the two families hold in the highest esteem. The husband offers his hand to a lady of consideration. Husband and wife dance the second *contredanse* together. After that the dancing is indiscriminate except that the bride selects her partners. At a *rendu de nòce* all the honors are bestowed on the newly-wed. They occupy the places of honor side by side. When established in their new home they should within six months give a dinner of ceremony to the two families and the wedding guests.

Courtesy at Home.—Never forget that you are the child of your father. Act toward him at twenty as you did at ten. Arriving at age does not give the right to fail toward him in respect to any form of politeness. The father never loses the right to exact from his children respect, submission and tender consideration. Close your eyes to his weaknesses. Flatter his tastes even at the expense of our own. Do not blush at his faults but seek to extenuate them. When he speaks, be silent. Mark his preferences and his prejudices, and do not wound them by thoughtless expressions. Give him your society if he needs it, and furnish him with whatever distraction is possible to you in old age and trouble. A child should be even more delicately attentive to his mother. He should avoid all contradiction, be always amiable and complaisant, and ever careful of her comfort and happiness. He should salute her kindly when he meets her in the morning and when he parts from her in the evening. Let her have the best place at the table and at the theater, in short surround her with unremitting attentions. Married sons and daughters should see their mother often, if it is possible. If not they should often express their remembrance of her by letters, messages, or gifts expressive of the love and esteem they bear for her. Grand-parents should be treated with respect, veneration even. Every opportunity should be sought to give them pleasure. Their advice should be listened to. Supply or supplement their weaknesses of age with your strength of youth. Sit with them read to them if necessary. To mock at old age is not only vicious but foolish, since to all persons it comes inevitably and comes so soon. To brothers and sisters be gentle, considerate, polite, just, free from rivalry, familiar and affectionate without undue familiarity. They should be held and regarded as the best and truest friends of a lifetime. Children should be treated with forbearance and polite consideration. No friend no matter how intimate should ever be treated with that familiarity which degenerates into impoliteness or breeds contempt. Servants and inferiors no matter of what class should be treated with polite consideration, teachers, by their pupils with love and veneration.

New Year Gratuities.—The following curious rules for bestowing gratuities at the beginning of the New Year are given by a French writer on good manners. They represent the common usage regarding the matter in Paris. Money is given to the concierge in proportion to the rent paid by the tenant; five francs for an apartment of less than five hundred francs; ten francs for an apartment costing from five hundred to eight hundred francs; twenty for one from eight hundred to fifteen hundred; twenty-five from fifteen hundred to two thousand, and so on adding five francs for each additional thousand francs of rent. When servants have been more than a year in service it is usual to give them a month's wages. When they have been in position a briefer time, they expect not more than twenty francs and not less than ten. It is the custom in many great country-houses to keep during the summer a box with an opening into which guests, on leaving, can put the gratuities intended for the servants. In this manner they are able to avoid imposition and give according to their means. A franc is given to the letter-carrier on New Year's day if one receives few letters, and from two to three if the correspondence is more important. A franc is given to newspaper-carriers. It is the custom in the provinces, though not in Paris, to make New Year's presents to servants at houses where one dines often. In the country one gives also something to the cook, to the chambermaid, and to those who wait at table. One gives to a gentleman's coachman if he has been conveyed to some place alone, but not if he has been so conveyed with the master.

Riding and Driving.—If you assist a lady to mount, hold your hand at a convenient distance from the ground that she may place her foot in it. As she springs, you aid her by the impetus of your arm. Practice only will enable you to do this properly. A gentleman, in riding with a lady, never permits her to pay the tolls. If good riding is necessary for a lady, it is, doubly so for a man. A gentleman's education cannot be called complete unless he can ride well. If this has been neglected early in life, no time should be lost in repairing the error. By riding first with a careful master for some months, and afterwards quite regularly alone, considerable proficiency may be attained even at a late period.

When attending a lady in a horseback ride, never mount your horse until she is ready to start. Give her your hand to assist her in mounting, arrange the folds of her habit, hand her her reins and her whip, and then take your own seat on your saddle.

Let her pace be yours. Start when she does, and let her decide how fast or slowly she will ride. Never let the head of your horse pass the shoulder of her, and be watchful and ready to render her any assistance she may require. Never, by rapid riding, force her to ride faster than she may desire.

Do not touch her bridle, reins, or whip, except she particularly requests your assistance, or an accident, or threatened danger, makes it necessary.

If there is dust or wind, ride so as to protect her from it as far as possible. If the road is muddy, be careful that you do not ride so as to bespatter her habit. It is best to ride on the side away from that on which her habit falls.

A man should be able to mount on either side of the horse. He places his left foot in the stirrup, his left hand on the saddle, and swings himself up, throwing his right leg over the horse's back. Nothing is more graceless than to see a man climb with both hands into his seat. A firm light seat is only learned by assiduous practice. The chief rules are to sit upright, but not stiffly, and well back in the saddle; to keep the knees pressed well in against the sides of the saddle, and the feet parallel to the horse's body; and to turn the toes in rather than out. The foot should be about half-way in the stirrup, which in long riding slips down to the hollow of the foot. The great desideratum in the art of riding is plenty of confidence. Of course a fearless rider can ride ungracefully, but no timid person can fail to be awkward.

In driving, again, there is a difference of style. The art is simple enough, but it requires practice. The good driver will understand the horse he has to drive, and will use him well, whether the beast be his own or another's. He will turn his corners gently or slowly, and will know when to put on the steam and when to turn it off. He will, of course, understand the management of his harness. Accidents may occur from the most trifling disarrangement of the harness, and no one should handle the reins who cannot harness and unharness a horse.

In the Carriage.—In the carriage a gentleman places himself with his back to the horses and leaves the best seat for the ladies. Only very elderly gentlemen are privileged to accept the best seat to the exclusion of young ladies. When the carriage stops the gentleman should alight first in order to assist the lady. To get in and out of a carriage gracefully is a simple but important accomplishment. If there is but one step, and you are going to take your seat facing the horses, put your left foot on the step and enter the carriage with your right in such a manner as to drop at once into your seat. If you are about to sit with your back to the horses reverse the process. As you step into the carriage be careful to keep your back towards the seat you are about to occupy so as to avoid the awkwardness of turning when once in. A gentleman cannot be too careful to avoid stepping on ladies' dresses when he gets in or out of a carriage. He should also beware of shutting them in with the carriage door. Never put your arm across the seat, or around her, as many do in riding. It is an impertinence which she would very properly resent as such.

Etiquette in Church.—If you visit other churches than your own, do not sneer or scoff at any of their forms, but follow the service as closely as you can.

To remove your hat, if a gentleman, upon entering church, is a sign of respect never to be omitted. Follow the customs of those around you.

A gentleman should pass up the aisle with the lady until he reaches the pew to be occupied, when he steps before her, opens the door, holds it open while she enters, and follows her, closing the door after him.

If you are visiting a strange church, request the sexton to give you a seat. Never enter a pew uninvited. If you are in your own pew in church, and see strangers looking for a place, open your pew door, and by a motion invite them to enter.

A gentleman or lady may offer a fan or book to a stranger near, if they are unprovided, whether they be young or old, lady or gentleman.

If you visit a church to see pictures or monuments and not for worship, choose the hours when there is no service being read. Speak low, walk slowly, and keep an air of quiet respect in the edifice.

Hanging around church doors and staring at the ladies, making remarks, is very ill-bred. If you are waiting to join any one, remain unobstrusive until they make their appearance, and then quietly rejoin them.

Hints to both Sexes.—All egotism must be banished from the drawing-room. The person who makes his family, his wealth, his affairs, or his hobby the topic of conversation, is not only a bore, but a violater of charity and good taste. We meet in society, not to make a display of ourselves, but to give and take as much rational entertainment as our own accomplishments and those of others can afford. He who engrosses the conversation is as unpardonably selfish, as he who allows his neighbor no elbow-room. The drawing-room is not a monarchy but a republic, where the rights of all are equal. Very young people should never be neglected. If we wish our sons and daughters to possess easy, polished manners, and fair powers of expressing themselves, we should treat them politely and kindly, and lead them to take an interest in whatever conversation may be going on. Neither must we bring our gloomy moods or irritable temper with us when we enter society. To look pleasant is a duty we owe to others. One is bound to listen with the appearance of interest to even the most inveterate proser who fastens upon us in society ; to smile at a twice-told tale ; and, in short, to make such minor sacrifices of sincerity, as good manners and good feeling demand. Awkwardness of attitude does one the same ill service as awkwardness of speech. Lolling, gesticulating, fidgetting, and the like, give an air of *gaucherie,* and, so to say, take off a certain percentage from the respect of others. A lady who sits cross-legged, or sideways on her chair, who has a habit of holding her chin, or twirling her watch chain—a man who sits across his chair, or bites his nails, or nurses his leg—manifests an unmistakable want of good breeding. Both should be quiet, easy, and graceful in their carriage; the man, of course, being allowed somewhat more freedom than the lady. If an object is to be indicated, you must move the whole hand, or the head, but never point with the finger. Coughing, sneezing, clearing the throat, &c., if done at all, must be done quietly. Sniffing, snuffing, expectorating, must never be performed in society under any consideration.

The Dress Coat.—The dress coat has a history dating back scarcely a hundred years. Its advent was immediately preceded by the long and highly ornamented waistcoat. It is said to have been first suggested by the turning back of the corners of the skirts of soldiers' coats to give greater freedom of movement, a style still seen in the military uniform of certain nations. It was first worn in France and soon afterwards introduced into England. It was elegant and convenient. It displayed the form and was not in the way in crowded assemblies or in ball-rooms. During the early part of the present century it was more cut away at the sides than at present. The collar was high and the skirts extremely narrow. Its color was usually blue and its buttons of brass. The grandfathers of the present generation wore it upon all occasions,

13

to balls, to parties, to church, in legislative halls and in the street. In fact it seemed to be nowhere inappropriate. It is hardly more than a quarter of a century since society began to be exacting in respect to the times and places where it should be worn, and the rules given by so-called authorities are still far from definite. On the continent of Europe it is much worn with a white vest, and a New York tailor ambitious of being an arbiter of fashion, has declared that it should so be worn in America. But good taste would seem to indicate that the white expanse of shirt-front displayed by a low-cut vest is sufficient without extending the desert of whiteness entirely to the waist. Some gentlemen affect a compromise of full dress by wearing a black tie with the dress-coat, but the narrow band of black seems out of place and conveys an impression of incompleteness. Some authorities say that the style is permissible at balls are parties, but not at the opera. The following suggestions convey as nearly as possible the opinions of the most reliable writers on etiquette. The dress-coat should never be worn at weddings or any kind of social gatherings before the dinner hour. Afternoon calls or New Year's calls should be made in a frock coat, neat necktie of some light and quiet color, and pantaloons not black but of some cheerful hue and pattern. The dress-coat should be worn at the opera, at dinner-parties and at all formal social gatherings after dinner, always with a narrow white linen or cambric tie, low-cut vest, black pantaloons and simple jewelry if jewelry is worn at all. A gentleman so dressed is above criticism if his clothes are of good material and well made. To wear with full dress a black necktie or white vest is to court comment these being variations of style which few writers on good breeding venture to recommend.

The Toothpick.—A writer on good manners who lived in the time of Charles the Second says, "Beware of rubbing your teeth with your napkin and picking them with your fingers." And again, when speaking of the toothpick, he adds, "When the cloth is taken away, it is not decent to pull a case of toothpicks out of your pocket." We hear even before this time how the Viscountess

Lisle "sends my toothpicker to the Palsgrave because when he was here I did see him wear a pen, or case, to pick his teeth with." From which we infer that the indecency of the public use of the toothpick had dawned on the minds of some persons in social position even in the unrefined eras of Elizabeth, James and the Charleses. The toothpick is a necessary but detestable implement which can only be used with propriety in dark corners and during unsocial moments. It should never be placed on dining-tables nor in conspicuous places, but in retired apartments where it can be employed without observation. The reasons for this are clean and obvious. They do not require to be elucidated, and they will not bear with decency any degree of appropriate illustration.

The Inside of the Walk.—The prejudice in favor of the "inside of the walk" is of distant origin. Two hundred years ago sidewalks were unknown. Streets sloped from the sides toward the center along which ran a stream conveying the drainage of the city to some convenient locality in the suburbs. For many hundred years pedestrians picked their way along the public thoroughfares clinging to the walls to avoid the unclean rivulet which flowed or stagnated in the middle of the street. Under these circumstances chivalrous gentlemen appearing with ladies in public naturally gave them the wall and took the chances of the gutter themselves. The first sidewalks were narrow, which caused a continuance of the practice. As they gradually broadened, as cities grew populous, and pedestrians increased in number, it became an imperative necessity that all should turn to the right regardless of sex. In fact, the inside of the walk with its cellar-doors and gratings had by this time become the most dangerous and difficult part of it. Hence the rule which governs well-bred pedestrians in all large cities. But while most persons yield a ready assent to it there are many who still cling to the idea that politeness requires the inside of the walk to be always given to ladies. It is an extraordinary case of survival of prejudice. It is true most of those who insist on taking the wall are servant girls or people from the country; but now and then a lady, so-called, is equally strenuous, and the result is sometimes an undignified collision. A gentleman dodging round on all sides of a lady and changing places with her at every street-corner is a most ridiculous spectacle. Instead of this a gentleman should always give his right arm to a lady with whom he is walking in the street, and maintain that relative position. Then as all turn to the right she is always protected, being never jostled by people going in the opposite direction. To observe any other rule than this is not only inconvenient for both lady and gentleman but troublesome to all other pedestrians.

These rules which apply to the boulevards and streets of American cities require some modification in their application to the narrow thoroughfares and inconvenient sidewalks that still exist in Paris and most European cities. If a gentleman is walking with a lady he is governed by circumstances. If on the inside of the walk she is better protected from pedestrians or passing vehicles it should be given her. If he is alone he should descend into the street rather than compel a lady to do so. The tendency in the crowded streets of Paris, even in the narrowest, is to turn to the right regardless of sex. Even for ladies it is usually less inconvenient. In the street ladies, in the matter of etiquette, are usually greater sinners than men, because too exacting. They should never occupy the *trottoir* in walking in two's or three's. If it rains they should be careful to keep the umbrella, if raised, from coming in contact with the hats of gentlemen, and if closed, should not carry it with the handle projecting at the side. A lady should observe the forms of politeness as scrupulously when abroad as when at home, which is unfortunately not always the case.

Smart Sayings.—The temptation of saying a smart and witty thing, or *bon mot*, and the malicious applause with which it is commonly received, have made people who can say them, and, still oftener, people who think they can, but cannot, and yet try, more enemies, and implacable ones too, than any one other thing that I know of. When such things, then, shall happen to be said at your expense (as sometimes they certainly will), reflect seriously upon the sentiments of uneasiness, anger and resentment, which they excite in you; and consider whether it can be prudent, by the same means, to excite the same sentiments in others, against you. It is a decided folly to lose a friend for a jest; but in my mind, it is not a much less degree of folly, to make an enemy of an indifferent and neutral person for the sake of a *bon mot*. When things of this kind happen to be said of you, the most prudent way is to seem not to suppose that they are meant at you, but to dissemble and conceal whatever degree of anger you may feel inwardly; and should they be so plain that you cannot be supposed ignorant of their meaning, to join in the laugh of the company against yourself; acknowledge the hit to be a fair one, and the jest a good one, and play off the whole thing in seeming good humor; but by no means reply in the same way; which only shows that you are hurt, and publishes the victory which you might have concealed. Should the thing said, indeed, injure your honor, or moral character, there is but one proper reply; which I hope you will never have occasion to make.—*Chesterfield.*

Temper.—The principal of these things is the mastery of one's temper, and that coolness of mind, and serenity of countenance which hinders us from discovering, by words, actions or even looks, those passions or sentiments by which we are inwardly moved or agitated; and the discovery of which gives cooler and abler people such infinite advantages over us, not only in great business, but in all the most common occurrences of life. A man who does not possess himself enough to hear disagreeable things, without visible marks of anger and change of countenance, or agreeable ones without sudden bursts of joy and expansion of countenance, is at the mercy of every artful knave, or pert coxcomb; the former will provoke or please you by design, to catch unguarded words or looks; by which he will easily decipher the secrets of your heart, of which you should keep the key yourself, and trust it with no man living.—*Chesterfield.*

How to Please.—An air, a tone of voice, a composure of coun-tenance to mildness and softness, which are all easily acquired, do the business; and without farther examination, and possibly with the contrary qualities, that man is reckoned the gentlest, the modestest, and the best natured man alive. Happy the man who, with a certain fund of parts and knowledge, gets acquainted with the world early enough to make it his bubble, at an age when most people are the bubbles of the world! for that is the common case of youth. They grow wiser when it is too late: and, ashamed and vexed at having been bubbles so long, too often turn knaves at last. Do not, therefore, trust to appearances and outside yourself, but pay other people with them, because you may be sure that nine in ten of mankind do, and ever will, trust to them. This is by no means a criminal or blamable simulation, if not used with an ill intention. I am by no means blameable in desiring to have other people's good word, good will, and affection, if I do not mean to abuse them. Your heart, I know, is good, your sense is sound, and your knowledge extensive. —*Chesterfield.*

Theatre Etiquette for Gentlemen.—In inviting a lady to accom-pany you to the theatre, opera, a concert, or any other public place of amusement, send the invitation the day previous to the one selected for taking her, and write it in the third person. If it is the first time you have invited her, include her mother, sister or some other lady in the invitation. If she accepts your invitation, let it be your next care to secure good seats. Although, when alone, you will act a courteous part in giving your seat to a strange lady, who is standing in a crowded concert-room, you should not do so when you are with a lady. By giving up your place beside her, you may place a lady next her, whom she will find an unpleasant companion, and you are yourself separated from her, when the conversation between the acts makes one of the greatest pleasures of an evening spent in this way. In case of accident, too, it gives her the appearance of having come alone. Your first duty when you are escorting a lady, is to the lady before all others.

When you are with a lady at a place of amusement, you must not leave your seat until you rise to escort her home. If at the opera, you may invite her to a promenade between the acts, but if she declines, you remain in your seat.

Let your conservation be in a tone that will not disturb those seated near you, unless you consider yourself part of the performance.

If the evening you have appointed be a stormy one, you must call for your companion with a carriage, and this is the more elegant way of taking her even if the weather does not make it absolutely necessary.

When you are entering a concert-room, or the box of a theatre, walk before your companion up the aisle, until you reach the seats you have secured ; then turn, offer your hand to her, and place her in the inner seat, taking the outside one yourself ; in going out, if the aisle is too narrow to walk two abreast, you again precede your companion until you reach the lobby, when you turn and offer your arm.

If your seats are secured, call for your companion in time to be seated three or four minutes before the performance commences ; but if you are visiting a hall where you cannot engage seats, it is best to go early.

If you are alone and see ladies present with whom you are acquainted, you may, with perfect propriety, go and chat with them between the acts, but when with a lady, never leave her to speak to another lady.

Never, unless urgently solicited, attach yourself to any party at a place of amusement, even if some of the members of it are your own relatives or intimate friends.

Miscellaneous Rules.—"Decorum," says a French writer, " is nothing less than the respect of one's self and others brought to bear upon every circumstance of life." In all relations, whether social or domestic, anything approaching coarseness, undue familiarity or levity of conduct is prolific of evil.

The proper giving and receiving of gifts may be almost styled an intuition which every one does not possess. A generous person may unwittingly wound where he intends to confer nothing but gratification. A grateful person may, through want of tact, seem almost to deprecate the liberality of the giver.

In society all should receive equal attention, the young as well as the old. The natural *gaucherie* of young girls results more from the slights which they are constantly receiving, and constantly expecting to receive, than from any real awkwardness inherent in their age.

Always give precedence to those older or of higher position than yourself unless they request you to take the precedence, when it is more polite to obey than to adhere to the strict rule of etiquette, since compliance with and adherence to the wishes of others display the finest breeding. In matters of precedence, be more careful to give others their rank than to take your own.

Always express your own opinions with modesty, and, if called upon, defend them, but without that warmth which may lead to hard feelings. Do not enter into argument. Having spoken your mind, and thus shown you are not cowardly in your beliefs or opinions, drop the subject and lead to some other topic. There is seldom any profit in discussion.

It is now entirely out of date to ask another at the dinner-table to drink wine with you. Each drinks at his own option, and as little as he chooses. If a person declines, he should by no means be pressed to take more. If he refuses to drink it altogether, he has a perfect right to do so, and no notice should be taken of the fact.

It is neither polite nor respectful to smoke in the presence of ladies, even though they have given permission. In truth, a gentleman will never ask such permission. Neither will he smoke in any room which ladies are in the habit of frequenting. This is etiquette but not comfort.

A gentleman may keep his hat on when handing a lady to a carriage, certain rules of etiquette to the contrary notwithstanding. Indeed, for him to do otherwise, and at the same time give proper assistance to the lady, he would find it necessary to have a dozen hands.

Never affect superiority. In the company of an inferior never let him feel his inferiority. If you invite an inferior as your guest, treat him with all the politeness and consideration you would show an equal. Assumption of superiority is the distinguishing trait of a parvenu.

Conform your conduct as far as possible to the company you chance to be with, only do not throw yourself into improper company. It is related of a certain king that he once turned his tea into a saucer and drank it thus because two country ladies whom he was entertaining did so. That king comprehended the true spirit of a gentleman. It is better even to laugh at and join in with vulgarity, so that it do not degenerate into indecency, than to set yourself up as better and better-mannered than those with whom you may chance to be associated. True politeness and genuine good manners often not only permit but absolutely demand a temporary violation of the ordinary obligations of etiquette.

Never address a mere acquaintance by his Christian name. He will have reason to take offense at your presumption. No lady will speak of a gentleman by his surname without the customary prefix of Mr.

Never speak of your husband or wife by their initial letter. Among very intimate friends it may be allowable to mention them by their Christian names, but among strangers and mere acquaintances they should always be referred to as Mr. or Mrs.——. It is not even allowable to mention them as "my wife" or "my husband."

"Civility," says Lord Chesterfield, "is particularly due to all women; and remember that no provocation whatsoever can justify any man in not being civil to every woman; and the greatest man would justly be reckoned a brute if he were not civil to the meanest woman. It is due to their sex, and is the only protection they have against the superior strength of ours."

Bishop Beveridge says, "Never speak of a man's virtues before his face or his faults behind his back."

Another maxim is, "In private watch your thoughts; in your family watch your temper; in society watch your tongue."

General salutations of the company are now wholly disused; in society, well-bred persons only recognize their own friends or acquaintances. If you are at the house of a new acquaintance, and find yourself among entire strangers, remember that, by so meeting under one roof, you are all in a certain sense made known to one another, and ought therefore to be able to converse freely, as equals. It is to be regretted that in the very highest circles the spirit of exclusiveness is still too strong to permit this; but still to shrink away to a side-table, and affect to be absorbed in some album or illustrated work, or to cling to some unlucky acquaintance, as a drowning man clings to a spar, are *gaucheries* no shyness can excuse. Neither should a man stand too long in the same spot. To be afraid to move from one drawing-room to another, is the sure sign of a neophite in society.

Be careful in company how you defend your friends, unless the conversation be addressed to yourself. Remember that nobody is perfect, and people may sometimes speak the truth; and that, if contradicted, they may be desirous of justifying themselves, and will *prove* what might otherwise have been a matter of doubt.

Never speak of your own children, except to your servants, as "Master" Tom or "Miss" Mary. Give them their Christian names only.

Remember in conversation that a voice "gentle and low" is, above all other extraneous accomplishments, "an excellent thing in woman." There is a certain distinct but subdued tone of voice which is peculiar only to persons of the best breeding. It is better to err by the use of too low than too loud a tone. Loud laughter is extremely objectionable in society.

SUPPLEMENTAL LIST OF NAMES AND ADDRESSES.

. . . .

Berger, Mr. and Mrs. L. S.; 45 r Jacques-Dulud (Neuilly).
Clarke, John, 1 r Lafayette
Clarke, Thomas S., 30 r Faubourg St. Honoré
Clarke, William, 1 r Lafayette
Deering, Dr. and Mrs. Benjamin ; bd Poissonnière
Delille, Edward; address 50 bd Haussmann
Espey, Edward; 48 r Faubourg St. Denis
Ferguson, B. F.; 38 bd St. Michel
Fuller, David T. C.; 24 r Pigalle
Herz, Mr. and Mrs. Cornelius; 37 ave Kleber
Hilton, J. B.; 24 r St. André-des-Arts
La Boissière, Count and Countess de; 7 r Provence
Limet, Félix; address 36 *bis* ave de l'Opéra
Morgan, Rev. Dr. and Mrs. John B.; 5 ave Montaigne
    Morgan, Miss
    Cowie, Miss
Mosler, Mr. and Mrs. Henry, Saturdays; 12 r La Trémoille
    Mosler, Arthur
Newbery, Mr. and Mrs. J. J.; 44 r Lacroix
    Newbery, J. C.
    Newbery. Miss
Rathbone, Mr. and Mrs. J. L.; address 24 r Quatre-Septembre

Roussey, Miss Henriette; 12 r Jouffroy
Salter, T. G.; address Munroe & Co.
Sanderson, Miss Sibyl; 30 r Bassano
  Sanderson, Miss
Smedley, William F., 30 r Faubourg St. Honoré
Tudor, Mr. and Mrs. William; 9 r des Beaux-Arts
Wynhamer, G. J.; 37 ave de Paris (Rueil)
  Wynhamer, Henry

AMERICAN JOURNALISTS IN PARIS.

Personnel of the Local Press.

American Register, 2 rue Scribe; Dr. Thomas W. Evans, Proprietor; Dr. E. A. Crane, Director of Editorial Department; O. C. Cunst, Editorial Writer.

Daily Morning News, 2 rue Scribe; Albert C. Ives, Director.

Galignani's Messenger, 224 rue Rivoli; Prof. Thomas Yeatman, American Editor.

American Messenger, 50 boulevard Haussmann; L. S. Berger & Co., Proprietors; Edward Delille, Editor.

Correspondents of American Journals.

Inman Barnard, New York *Herald.*
Miss Bullet, Brooklyn *Eagle.*
Theodore Chase, New York *Sun.*
Mrs. Crawford, New York *Tribune.*
Henry Haynie, Boston *Herald,* San Francisco *Chronicle.*
Mrs. Lucy Hooper, Philadelphia *Telegraph,* St. Louis *Post-Dispatch.*
Edward King, New York *Evening Post,* Boston *Journal.*
Baroness Salvador, New York *World.*
Theodore Stanton, Chicago *Interocean.*
Albert Sutliffe, San Francisco *Chronicle.*
Carroll Tevis, New York *Times.*

PLACES OF INTEREST TO TOURISTS.

It must be taken for granted that Americans coming to Paris desire to see those things that interest tourists in general, that

is to say the palaces, the museums, the picture-galleries, the parks and gardens, the churches, the famous cemeteries, the antiquities.

They naturally feel some curiosity regarding places made memorable by the presence of the great men of our revolutionary

period, such as Franklin, Jefferson, Monroe, and Gouverneur Morris, and the distinguished Frenchmen, such as Lafayette, who

were our friends at the same epoch. Lafayette's residence in the rue d'Anjou is a place of pilgrimage shown by the guides. A

house associated with the name of Franklin is in the rue Penthièvre. That which he occupied at Passy during the eight years

of his stay in France has been torn down but the one adjoining it remains. Nothing remains to indicate the house in the Cul-de-

sac Têtebout (now the rue Taitbout) occupied by Jefferson, first minister of the United States to France. Other houses occupied

by the American Ministers who immediately succeeded him have
in the course of time lost their identity. Places connected with

Diner Européen, 14 bd des Italiens.

the massacre of St. Bartholomew and Henry IV. are interesting
to Americans. Such are the window on the side of the Louvre

Harvey, English Electro-Plate and Silverware, etc., 23 bd des Capucines.

facing the quay from whose balcony Charles IX. is said to have
fired at the Protestants attempting to escape; the church of

John Ehrendall, American Tailor, 50 rue Chaussée d'Antin.

St. Germain l'Auxerrois the first to sound the tocsin; the clock
then in the tower of this church, but now in a tower of the

Pension de Famille, rue Molitot, Passy.

Palais de Justice which marked the hour for the beginning of the
massacre; the room in the Louvre where Henry IV. died, and the

Joseph Williamson, Manufacturing Jeweller, 7 rue Castiglione.

place where he was assassinated by Ravaillac in the rue
St. Honoré in front of No. 3, the house being now demolished.

Champagne de Venoge & Co., 5 rue Scribe.

The places where persons celebrated in history or literature have
lived will also be visited. Among the resorts of Americans are

Rudy Institute, 7 rue Royale.

the banks where they do business, at which are reading-rooms, the
American Exchange, and the Institute Rudy, often visited for

J. D. Stickney, American Guide, 1 rue du Havre.

its public entertainments. There is here an operatic class where
instruction is given in respect to matters pertaining to the stage.

Mme. Duperon, Kiosque No. 12, bd des Capucines.

200

14

ANCHOR LINE
UNITED STATES MAIL STEAMERS.

LIVERPOOL AND NEW YORK
Via Queenstown.

EXPRESS SERVICE
S.S. "CITY OF ROME," 8415 Tons

This magnificent Steamship will sail to and from above Ports at regular intervals

Saloon Fares, £12 12 to £26 5.

GLASGOW TO NEW YORK (via Moville)
EVERY THURSDAY

Saloon Fares, £9 9 to £15 15.

For Freight and Passage apply to Messrs. HENDERSON BROTHERS, Liverpool: 17, Water Street; London: 18, Leadenhall Street and 8, Regent Street; Glasgow: 49, Regent Street

OR

3, RUE SCRIBE, PARIS

THE COMMERCIAL CABLE COMPANY
(MACKAY-BENNETT CABLES)

The only Company having a Cable running direct into New York City, thus rendering this

THE QUICKEST AND MOST RELIABLE ROUTE BETWEEN EUROPE AND AMERICA

Special Wire from Havre to Paris and direct Wires from Havre to Principal Continental Cities.

Telegrams marked " VIA COMMERCIAL " may be handed in at any Continental or British Telegraph Office.

Head Offices { Continent: 26, AVENUE DE L'OPÉRA, PARIS.
England: 23, ROYAL EXCHANGE, LONDON.

CHAMPAGNE WINES

MOËT AND CHANDON

ONLY DEPOT IN PARIS, 8, PLACE DE L'OPÉRA

P. GUIBERT, Agent

DRY WINES TO SUIT AMERICAN TASTE

BRUT-IMPERIAL. *CREMANT BLANC (White Seal).*

MISS ANNA E. KLUMPKE
Studio, 8, Rue de la Grande Chaumière, Paris

PORTRAITS A SPECIALTY

LIMITED NUMBER OF PUPILS TAKEN

Geneva

Nonmagnetic Watch Company.

LOUIS BORNAND, AGENT.

5, Quai du Mont-Blanc   GENEVA

(Switzerland)

———— ✤ ————

AMERICAN READING ROOM

GENEVA (SWITZERLAND)

5, Quai du Mont - Blanc

Leading American papers received direct. Letters sent to visitors care of American Reading Room, 5, Quai du Mont-Blanc, received and cared for.

JOHN EHRENDALL

American Tailor

20, Rue de la Chaussée d'Antin, 20

PARIS

PENSION DE FAMILLE

Rue Molitot, Passy.

BEST HOME COMFORTS — LOW RATES

EXCELLENT REFERENCES

BEST SITUATION IN PARIS

AMERICAN DENTAIRE

(THUS DENOMINATED EXPRESSLY ON ACCOUNT OF ITS FRANCO-AMERICAN FORMATION)

1, RUE LAFAYETTE, PARIS

Founded by an American Company, contains over twenty rooms, attended by eminent American Dentists. Every branch of Dental Art such as (1) Fillings, (2) Replacing of Lost Teeth, (3) Extraction, (4) Straightening of Teeth, (5) Obturation of the Palate of the Mouth, is performed by a Specialist, so that attendance is given by men possessing perfect knowledge of their art and of the most recent inventions.

Diseases of the Mouth and Tumors of the Gums are cared for by a Medical Doctor of the Paris Faculty, who is Director of the House.

AMERICAN DENTAIRE has suppressed putting to sleep by "Laughing Gas," which may produce mortal accidents. By a simple application to the tooth of an inoffensive liquid, "The Alpine," (exclusive property of the Company) roots are extracted without pain and without that necessity.

PRICES ARE RIGOROUSLY FIXED, AND ARE AS LOW AS COM-PATIBLE WITH CONSCIENCIOUS WORKMANSHIP AND FIRST-CLASS MATERIAL

Gold Fillings. . . . . Fr.	10
Platina and Enamel	5
Extractions, simple	3
„ with " Alpine "	8
Plates, 1 tooth	10
Complete Set, upper and lower (28 teeth) . . .	150

WORKMANSHIP GUARANTEED.   NO WAITING.

1, Rue Lafayette, Paris

208

www.ingramcontent.com/pod-product-compliance
Lightning Source LLC
Chambersburg PA
CBHW071946110426
42744CB00030B/549